THE EVOLUTION
OF THE LIBERAL DEMOCRATIC STATE
WITH A CASE STUDY
OF LATINOS IN SAN ANTONIO, TEXAS

THE EVOLUTION
OF THE LIBERAL DEMOCRATIC STATE
WITH A CASE STUDY
OF LATINOS IN SAN ANTONIO, TEXAS

Henry Flores

Studies in Political Science
Volume 9

The Edwin Mellen Press
Lewiston•Queenston•Lampeter

Library of Congress Cataloging-in-Publication Data

Flores, Henry.
    The evolution of the liberal democratic state with a case study of latinos in San Antonio,
Texas / Henry Flores.
        p. cm. -- (Studies in political science ; v. 9)
    Includes bibliographical references and index.
    ISBN 0-7734-6674-6 (hc)
        1. Mexican Americans--Texas--San Antonio--Politics and government. 2. San Antonio
(Tex.)--Politics and government. 3. Mexican Americans--Texas--San Antonio--Social
conditions. 4. San Antonio (Tex.)--Ethnic relations. 5. Democracy--Case studies. I. Title.
II. Studies in political science (Lewiston, N.Y.) ; v. 9.

    E184.M5F58 2003
    320.9764'351--dc21

                                                                                                    2003046480

This is volume 9 in the continuing series
Studies in Political Science
Volume 9 ISBN 0-7734-6674-6
SPSc Series ISBN 0-7734-7434-X

A CIP catalog record for this book is available from the British Library

The Edwin Mellen Press   The Edwin Mellen Press
Box 450   Box 67
Lewiston, New York   Queenston, Ontario
USA 14092-0450   CANADA L0S 1L0

The Edwin Mellen Press, Ltd.
Lampeter, Ceredigion, Wales
UNITED KINGDOM SA48 8LT

Printed in the United States of America

Dedication

To my wife and colleague, Gwen, who gave me the intellectual spark and encouragement necessary to the completion of this book. And, to Julia, my daughter who had the patience to understand the pressures I was going through in writing this work.

Table of Contents

Preface

In *The Evolution of the Liberal Democratic State With a Case Study of Latinos in San Antonio, Texas* Professor Henry Flores challenges conventional wisdom about the nature of the local state and critiques theories which describe urban political regimes as either static, autonomous entities, or as responsive democratic communities. He argues that the local state is best understood as a resistant *dynamical* system, adapting over time to changing political conditions, but generally preserving underlying patterns of social, economic, and political power.

To build his argument, Flores considers in turn the general condition of local democracy in the United States, patterns of class, ethnic and racial subordination in San Antonio, Texas, and the boundaries of Latino political empowerment. In the book's most innovative contribution, Professor Flores applies insights of chaos theory, drawn from the physics of fluid dynamics, treating the state as a complex system of energetic, dynamic entities which can be bounded, canalized, or blocked altogether. He is not the first social scientist to apply theories from the contemporary natural sciences, to questions of individual and social behavior, but you will find his application of these concepts unusually clear, providing a surprisingly close fit to empirical evidence about local development policy in San Antonio.

Fundamental Questions

For students and lay readers, *The Evolution of the Liberal Democratic State With a Case Study of Latinos in San Antonio, Texas* asks that you reconsider fundamental questions about politics in the United States. Is the U.S. actually a democracy? Are local states, in the form of municipal governments, responsive to new racial and ethnic constituencies? Will growing Latino populations attain political influence matching their numbers?

For political theorists and analysts, this book brings new arguments to the debate on the nature of the state. Should we think of the state as an autonomous, bounded entity, comprised of the institutions of government? In this view, all the elements of public power, financed by the public treasury and exercising authority in the name of the polity, including administrative agencies, courts, and legislatures — and all of the personnel who staff these institutions — *are* the state. But as Flores argues, urban social theories grounded in a static view of state institutions are hampered by their poor fit with the actual history of local regimes, which are characterized by nearly constant change.

A dynamic theory of the state, accommodating empirical knowledge about the creation and destruction of urban institutions, built environments, and political traditions, would more closely reflect the lived experience of urban residents, and capture more fully the nuances of urban political change, than neo-Weberian approaches premised on institutional rigidity, or neo-Marxist approaches which presuppose bourgeois hegemony. Neither approach accounts very well for the diversity, and the fluidity, of urban politics in the United States.

Federalism, Immigration, and Civil Rights

In the United States, urban institutional change has been conditioned by the unusual status of municipal government. Cities are simultaneously the level of politics most proximate to citizens and corporations, thus facing constant pressure from below, *and* the level most distant from financial and political resources of the national government. The consolidation of the U.S. national state, concurrent with the emergence of a national economic system, integrated capital markets, and technologies of communication and administration, have left cities vulnerable to economic dislocation and political neglect. This is ironic, because cities have historically been home to both industrial power and the bulk of the nation's population.

Cities have also been ports of entry and primary sites of employment, for successive generations of immigrant workers and their families. In principle, cities in the U.S. might thus have become — and to a certain extent actually are — political spaces where the democratic experiment could succeed most completely. Densely populated, more easily organized communities; diverse, tolerant metropolitan cultures; and large numbers of potential voters, all might have made cities powerful engines of democratic political development as well as regions of economic production.

Since World War II the racial and ethnic transformation of U.S. cities, characterized by racially-segregated suburbanization and corresponding inner-city concentration of African American, and to some extent Latino, populations, combined with political gains of the late 20th century civil rights movements, have created political opportunities for growing urban communities of color. These opportunities have resulted in the election and consolidation of urban regimes dominated by African American and Latino officials. Yet as Flores documents in the case of San Antonio, and as others have discovered for other U.S. cities, the *potential* empowerment of communities of color appears not to have resulted in major policy gains for those communities.

Chaos and Social Control

This suggests another paradox. If the state is dynamical, and demographic shifts are transforming urban populations and electorates, even minimal opportunities for democratic control should result in significant change, bringing urban policy — especially economic policy — more fully in line with the expectations of urban populations, even when those populations, as in San Antonio, have become predominantly Hispanic.

Yet the extensive empirical evidence Flores presents tells a very different story. In his narrative, the power struggle over control of the public policy agenda is one in which San Antonio's Mexican American communities have nearly always been the losers. It appears that the state, a *structural matrix* of interrelated institutions and processes, cannot be fully described as a collection of people, buildings, and equipment, even if we understand those institutions to be changeable. The local state in the U.S. incorporates an ideological value system — liberal democracy — which constrains its capacity for systemic change, beyond the traditional boundaries limiting public power vis-à-vis private enterprise.

The local state thus does appear capable of response and adaptation over time, giving it a dynamic character, *not* in order to more fully represent the interests of workers, their families, and their communities, even when those communities are politically mobilized, but to *prevent* that very mobilization from fundamentally altering existing distributions of power and wealth, reflected in the configuration of urban policy, governmental structure, and physical space. Thus the local state is a dynamic system, but it is a *resistant* system.

Comparative Implications and General Theories

As you read *The Evolution of the Liberal Democratic State With a Case Study of Latinos in San Antonio, Texas* you will surely find that your existing views of its central subjects — theories of the state, patterns of local democracy, Latino politics, and the potential empowerment of disempowered communities in U.S. cities — will be changed. You may also be encouraged to wonder whether these insights are generalizable, and can be applied to cities elsewhere in the world. How would Professor Flores' theories of dynamic structuralism, bounded local democracy, and ethnic subordination (within democratic institutions), be reflected in the local politics of very different social and political systems? How might they apply to places where local elites influence the local state not only through economic power, but also through religious, ethnic, or tribal institutions? Would the same general rules describe the conditions facing a local polity in Africa, Asia, or Latin America, caught between the power of a hegemonic national regime on the one hand, and the pervasive influence of the emerging global politico-economic system on the other? How could a dynamic structural perspective be used to better understand the politics of entirely new political systems in Russia, the other former Soviet republics, and Eastern Europe? In the neo-theocratic local polities of South Asia and the Middle East? For that matter, would the same principles apply elsewhere in the U.S., in the somewhat different political traditions which prevail in other regions of the country?

As you will soon discover, Professor Flores has written a book which asks you to think more deeply and more critically about what it means to be a citizen in the United States. Building on a careful review of contemporary urban social theory, and a detailed empirical analysis of San Antonio's development policy and history, *The Evolution of the Liberal Democratic State With a Case Study of Latinos in San Antonio, Texas* provides ample arguments and evidence to conclude that there is a great deal we do not know, and do not understand, about our own social, economic, and political realities. Beyond the many answers he provides, Professor Flores also offers the most important gift any political theorist can give to you, the reader: His book challenges you, and with its creative insights, prepares you, to ask all the right, critical questions about political democracy, social justice, and the obligations of informed citizenship.

Tony Affigne
Providence College
Rhode Island
January 2003

Acknowledgements

I would like to thank St. Mary's University who provided me with both sabbatical support and Faculty Development Grants throughout the time that I was composing this book. Additionally the encouragement of Gwen Diaz, Amy Bridges, Rudy Torres, Manny Avalos, and Charlie Cotrell have sustained me through the long years that were needed to organize my thoughts, construct the framework and complete the work on this manuscript. My appreciation is also extended to Gerry Frost for her creativity and patience in producing the cover for this volume. Without the intellectual and emotional support I received from each and every one of these good people this work would never have been completed.

An Essay on the State

Introduction

This book is about the "Theory of the State," the liberal democratic state, and how Latinos fare, socially and politically, as subjects of the state. More specifically, this book is about the local state, the government and politics of San Antonio, Texas, and how the policy apparatuses affect the political lives of its Latino residents.

The political condition of Latinos in the United States has been, continues to be, and will be the direct result of how the liberal democratic state is structured and functions bureaucratically and politically. The ideological mechanisms, that massive socialization structure that dictates the direction of thought and culture in any society, of a liberal democratic society dictate the various ways in which Latinos are perceived socially and politically. This perception becomes imbedded in the political and decisional processes of the state's structure resulting in the creation and implementation of public policies negatively affecting Latinos. Additionally, an equally discriminatory electoral process that makes it extremely difficult for Latinos to substantively affect those same policies undergirds discriminatory policies in areas such as economic development and education. The developmental and educational policies help in perpetuating the lower social status of Latinos in the United States. At the same time the electoral structures and processes are designed to inhibit the political participation of Latinos. This is particularly true in the city of San Antonio, Texas.

The State

Although much has been said and debated concerning the conceptual nature of the state the discussions have never reached a satisfactory conclusion. This will not occur until all parties agree on "a theory of the State." In other words, past and current debates of the state or aspects of the state, such as the extent or existence of the state's autonomy or the limits of the state, must be traced to the manner in which the state is conceptualized. This essay is not intended to settle any debate concerning the state or to propose "the Theory of the State." Rather, this is intended as "an essay" on the State that will contribute some different thoughts on the State's conception.

The specific questions that will be addressed in this essay are:

- Why does the state take the specific form that it does?
- What constitutes the "form" of the State?
- And, does the form of the State change throughout history and, if it does, what causes or factors determine and cause this change?

It appears that much of the recent controversy surrounding the state turns on the failure to agree on some fundamental issues relating to the state's parameters. Essentially, the concerns center on whether one level of conceptualization is more appropriate than another; whether the state possesses any "limits;" whether the state has a structure; and, whether that structure must be specific or take a specific form? All of these issues or questions arose in the "Controversy" between Bertell Ollman and Timothy Mitchell entitled "Going Beyond the State?" in the December 1992 issue of the <u>American Political Science Review</u>. These issues are not new, just more precisely articulated, but first arose in the now famous debates that raged during the 1970s between Nicos Poulantzas and Ralph Miliband. Miliband's argument assumed that the state's structure was benign, at least not biased ideologically; but that the individuals who controlled and manipulated the state designed and implemented policies favorable to the interests of those they served, whether they represented capital or labor. Poulantzas, on the other hand, believed that the state's structures and any structural arrangements were imbued with the ideological values of capitalism and, regardless of the best intentions on the part of any political actor, caused all important policy decisions to be oriented toward the general interests of capitalism.

Regardless, in order to appropriately address the above questions it appears that one may wish to begin by making the following assumptions.

1. The state may be spoken of on both abstract and concrete levels of conceptualization.

2. On an abstract level, the state can be treated as a complex matrix of interacting structures and processes.

3. Also on the abstract level, the state can be treated as a dynamical system.

4. As a complex and dynamic system the state's parameters must be considered flexible, amorphous, and constantly in flux.

5. The state, as a complex and dynamical system, likewise is composed of other complex and dynamical systems interacting with each other on many abstract and concrete levels.

Conceiving of the state as a dynamical system will allow for a more clear understanding of how the state is structured, the manner in which it is structured, and how and why it evolves from one form to another.

Until recently the state has always been conceived of as a "static" construct, however, this is not accurate in light of the fact that the various state structures and governing processes are constantly changing. On a concrete level this is best exemplified by looking at the way in which the American national government has evolved and grown over the last two hundred and twenty plus years. For that matter, any current city government does not look anything like it did when it was first created. The present day structures and structural arrangements, of both the American national and many local governments, reflect an evolutionary process triggered by many social, economic, and political forces that function throughout the structures. On some occasions these forces have arisen as a result of the internal dynamics of the state, on others external forces have caused the effects. Assuming that the state is static can falsely result in the conclusion that the state can or could never change, an empirical impossibility. On the other hand, if one views the state as a dynamical system then one can lend some theoretical understanding as to why and how the American national, or any other government, evolved into the entity it has become today.

Conceiving of the state as a dynamical system, subject to many and varied evolutionary forces, and changing through the course of time, is not a new or novel idea. Karl Marx alluded to the notion that during any particular historical era, characterized by a specific mode of production, a unique type of state would have to exist in order to organize society around that mode.[1] Fredrich Engels was more specific when he stated in his On the Origin of the Family, Private Property and the State (1884) that the state was a product of society at a certain stage of development. In other words, the forms and structures of the state change as the material or concrete and objective relations of a society and the modes of production change. This is necessary to insure the protection of the hegemonic position of the class who controls society's modes of production. These structural and systemic changes occur throughout the history and life of any given society. The structural changes are evident in the decisional processes and structures of the state resulting in the formation and implementation of public policy. Additionally, the changes also occur throughout the socialization processes particularly those producing the ideological legitimation holding a society together.

Lest the notion of a changing state be credited solely to the fathers of Marxism it should be noted that even Adam Smith, in his Wealth of Nations, concluded that for capitalism to thrive a specific state type was required. Although Smith did not elaborate on the specificity of a state form governing a capitalist society, several of his loyal adherents did including Jeremy Bentham,

---

[1] Although Marx did not specifically speak to the evolutionary process of the state he characterizes the state as different during the feudal and mercantilist eras. See his Pre-Capitalist Economic Formations (1964).

James and John Stuart Mill (Lustig, 1982; Rosenblum, 1987, and MacPherson, 1977).

Jeremy Bentham, writing at the dawn of industrial capitalism and during the beginning of the end of mercantile capitalism, felt that the control of the state by the old aristocracy could not provide the protection required by the social classes who would be the principle participants in the "new" economic world. The diffusion of private property into more and more hands required a state apparatus that would accommodate broader diversity of interests and, most importantly, the attendant social changes caused by the transference of social control between those classes. Furthermore, control of the state must pass into the hands of those who understood the "social psychology" of the new economy—the "novi homini," the new "middle class man." The complex and diverse nature of the economy required an equally complex and diverse state having both law making and adjudication institutions. These institutions had to be prepared to pass, interpret, and enforce laws that would provide legal protection for the broad, diverse groups acting in the new world of capitalism. These institutions also had to pass laws that would accommodate the many social changes resulting from the operation of a completely new and different mode of production (Rosenblum, 1978).

Essentially, a capitalist social system required a specific form of a state in order to function properly. Whatever the physical characteristics comprising this state the most important were conceptual in nature. For instance, it appears that Bentham and the two Mills felt that a liberal democratic state would have to be fragmented structurally and limited in power in order to prevent arbitrariness, such as the irrational or self-interested dictates of one person or group, from infecting the public policy process. The fragmented nature of the state apparatus, on the other hand, also would inhibit the ability of small groups or politically weak groups from ever gaining control of the entire structure. Additionally, a state having limited powers could also protect the sanctity of the property relations extant in a capitalist society insuring that the state could do very little in the manner of "curing" the material inequalities naturally arising within a capitalist society.

Nevertheless, not until Kennedy came forth with his The Rise and Fall of Great Powers (1987) was there any extended discussion of the state as a changing entity. Kennedy suggested that a state changed structures as a result of its efforts to expand itself economically and politically. The state's expansion could also lead eventually to its demise, its deconstruction—growth would result in what Kennedy labeled "overreach." This overextension would place so much tension on the state's ability to support itself that crises would ensue resulting in the collapse of the state. Fundamentally, the state grows itself beyond its capabilities to adequately nurture its population and, instead of growing, shrinks and, in some cases, passes out of existence altogether. The only other study attempting to investigate the changing state, Causes and Consequences of Changes in the State, appeared in 1990 edited by Edward Greenberg. Greenberg interpreted the types of changes that occurred in the state by utilizing three different types of theoretical models. Variously, change was attributed to the actions of individual political actors, social forces, or the effects of a society's or state's structures. Greenberg indicated that the forces or factors that caused change to occur varied depending upon which model one used. Still, by the end of his work the same questions remained that arose in the Ollman/Mitchell debate and they remained unanswered.

Why and how a state changes form from one historical era to another and within each historical era can best be explained by assuming that the state is by its very nature, dynamical. This assumption grew out of two theories arising from the world of the hard sciences—Chaos Theory and the Theory of Complexity. Although some, principally Glieck (1987), Kellert (1993), and Lorenz (1993), indicated that one cannot borrow theories from the sciences and apply them to social phenomenon, it will become clear by the end of this volume that they were not completely accurate. Many of the principles that comprise chaos theory are quite evident in the social world, this also will become clear when they are discussed in Chapter One.

Chaos Theory, which is not what it was originally called, was concocted in order to lend some understanding to the behavior of complex systems, specifically weather patterns. It is my contention that states are complex systems, albeit not as complex as weather systems, nevertheless complex. States are complex because of the fact that they are comprised of a multitude of humans whose behavior can only partially be predicted and whose behavior is dictated by both factors under and outside their control. More often than not, individual political actors are forced to behave in a way in which they do not wish due to already existing social conditions created by predecessors or by political actors from other systems that limit decisional options or policy possibilities. This is not to say that individuals cannot make an independent, rational, or responsible decision. Individual decisions, however, are predicated upon a set of choices limited by the political, social, and ideological parameters of a liberal democracy. This latter situation is unique to social rather than physical systems and represents a modification of chaos theory. Physicists exclude the possibility of a system being affected by outside factors apparently assuming that although there are finite limits on microphysical systems, these same systems are included in one system where the parameters are defined as infinite. On a macro-level this appears to make perfect sense and if applicable to social systems would offer the answer to the question concerning "whither the limits of the state?" There simply would be none! Nevertheless, at the micro-level of analysis one must necessarily assume that states, because they are artificial constructs, must have limits and, consequently, can be affected by outside forces. Complicating matters is the notion that the parameters of the state overlap those of other states particularly in a federated system or structure such as that existing in the United States of America.

Some additional arguments that complicate this discussion include many of the concerns mentioned by Ollman and Mitchell in their exchange particularly the notion that the state in American society is class based and is dominated by the interests of a specific class. Here there must be the consideration that general policy alternatives, considered and promulgated by the state benefit the general interests of the dominant class and are oriented in such a manner as to reproduce the class-based nature of capitalist society. Finally, the type of capitalist society that predominates in the United States is uniquely "American" in that as the state takes on a more dominant role in the economic processes of this society, there is a unique and sophisticated method for suppression of opposition to state policies. The media is utilized as an extension of the state apparatus to extend the span of control of the state over every sector of society.

Mitchell, however, departs from Ollman accusing him of reification and overstating the effectiveness of the state in the accumulation process. In Mitchell's perception, the subordination of the state to the capital accumulation process, appears to give conceptual priority to the process which, in turn, tends to hide the "incoherencies and fissures" in the state structures and processes. Additionally, Mitchell points out, rightfully so, that by subordinating the state to the accumulation process Ollman has opted for a macro-level of analysis while ignoring the possibility that many other levels, or combinations of levels of analysis, are possible. For instance, the possibility of conceptualizing a relationship between the micro and macro-levels of analysis is ignored resulting in overlooking the possibility that a micro-level accumulation effect may result in structural arrangements at the macro-level and vice-versa. Mitchell feels that by addressing the structural characteristics of the state this discussion can be better substantiated.

Perhaps both Ollman and Mitchell are correct to a certain extent. It appears that the capitalist state is such because it was formed with the purpose in mind to supervise social relations within and for a capitalist society. Consequently, the state's apparatuses have been fought over by those wishing to dominate both the class relations and the productive and reproductive processes of the state (Miliband, 1969). The struggle for control over the state apparatuses, however, has resulted in the creation of structures specifically designed to manage

xiv

a capitalist society (Poulantzas, 1978). Therefore, embedded in the state's structures are the guiding values and ideologies of capitalism. This notion will be discussed in Chapters One and Two of this volume, however, two brief examples are warranted here.

Charles Beard, the eminent historian, first discussed the notion that the national level of government was constructed specifically to protect the interests of the "Constitutional Fathers." Beard presented a detailed discussion of the backgrounds of the framers pointing out that one of the factors that tied these individuals together was that they held the national debt bonds of the Continental Congress. They protected their interests by writing into the "new" constitution a provision that the new government would honor that debt. The framers literally constitutionally guaranteed their interests requiring the new government to create a bureaucratic structure to repay the debt. This first step laid the groundwork for how this new state would come to be manipulated and oriented over the next two hundred years. On a theoretical level the framer's manipulation resulted in the creation of a state structure so complex and byzantine that it would be unable to address social, political, and economic problems that may arise at any one time.

The state eventually evolved into a web-like structure, where the legislature, executive, and judicial branches balanced and checked each other. This complex structure, in turn, was legitimated by an electoral process designed to make it difficult for the average citizen to both run for office and, in some cases, vote. The electoral process is designed, in order to limit access to control of the governmental structures and to allow only those individuals, ideologically acceptable, to seek elected office. This controls the passage, implementation, and interpretation of national and local policies that are favorable to the general interests of capital and against those of the working, low-income, poor classes, and racial minority groups.

At the local level the ideological orientation of the manner in which governments plan the use of land for economic development insures the maintenance of existing social relations. The scope and pace of the developmental plans eliminate participation by the small players while only providing more jobs for construction and service workers. The winners in local developmental efforts always appear to be developers and financiers while the losers are the displaced residents, temporary or seasonal and service workers, and taxpayers.

Embedded within the state structures are the decisional processes that create the policies promoting and maintaining the accumulation processes and existing social relations. The operations of these processes will be the focus of Chapters Two and Four. Nevertheless, both structures and processes are necessary to an appropriate conceptualization of the capitalist state because without them no linkage can be made between Ollman's and Mitchell's perceptions. Ollman is correct in stating that the state must be unique to a capitalist society while Mitchell is correct in stating that this uniqueness can be uncovered by including a discussion of the structures specific to the capitalist state.

Ollman's position that the capitalist state is unique to capitalist society, i.e. the state governing the Unites States of America is unique to the United States, is accurate. Varieties of liberal democracies abound, each uniquely born out of and formed by the history and culture of a specific country. So that if any "theory of the state" is to be constructed then it must be understood that it include this provision. Finally, "a theory of the state" should then be constructed that discusses general principles, qualities, or characteristics that comprise a state within a liberal democracy.

Latinos – The Data

The data that will form the empirical base for this essay will be the manner in which the state interacts with and affects the daily existence of Mexican Americans in San Antonio, Texas. The primary reason that this discussion is limited to Mexican Americans as opposed to an all-inclusive "Latino approach" is primarily one of personal choice. It has been my life-long suspicion that one of the chief barriers to the advancement of Mexican Americans in the United States has been because of the machinations of a state dominated by the interests of capital. The effects of racism, within the parameters of the model I present here, are the general result of the ideological creation and maintenance systems governing the social interactions within a liberal democracy. I strongly agree with Cornel West when he suggested that the social conditions that persons of color find themselves in are the consequence of factors that include racism (West, 1993). Racism is a manifestation of deep underlying structural mechanisms operating normally in a liberal democracy. The state and society generally manipulate the issue of race, in the creation and interpretation of public policy decisions, decisions that reinforce the social inequities confronting Mexican Americans daily. I suspect, however, that much of what I have concluded concerning the state induced socio-political conditions of Mexican Americans can also be said about other oppressed groups of Americans such as African Americans, Native Americans, women, gays, the working class, and other Latinos. Regardless, my perception of the relationship between the liberal democratic state and Mexican Americans represents a different perception, if not a different paradigm, from which to discuss Latino Politics. So, in this respect, the ideological "god-parents" of my work, besides the Marxists, structuralists, and chaos theoreticians, include all the work produced by scholars on Latino Politics.

The case studies on economic development and the electoral process were chosen because, like any "jigsaw puzzle," they represent public policy arenas that directly affect the Latino community. Superficially, the three policy areas appear unrelated and are generally treated separately in most academic circles. The complex nature of the state, however, causes these three policy areas to intricately relate. So that economic development provides the foundation for property wealth that, in turn, provides the revenue base for public education which, in turn, pays for public education. The electoral process allows Latinos access to the developmental process by gaining seats on both the city council and various boards and commissions. A systematic look at each of these policy arenas provides a glimpse at how Latinos are systemically excluded from the public policy decisional arenas. The exclusion occurs ideologically and structurally in that the interests of the Latino community are generally not essential elements in the economic development planning process. Concomitantly, Latinos are excluded from participation in the decisional structures because they are not elected to office consistently due to the racially polarized nature of the electorate and the electoral barriers that have consistently been placed before them inhibiting their participation.

The general economic development planning process of San Antonio, Texas is presented in Chapter Four to determine the effects of the decisional process on the general economic well being of the city's Latino community. This city was chosen because it is one of the largest cities in the United States possessing a significantly large Mexican origin population. Additionally, San Antonio possesses the largest most politically successful Mexican American middle class, proportionally, than any other city in the United States. As a result San Antonio's Latino population has been more electorally successful than any other Latino community in the United States. San Antonio provides a prime example for a "brief look" at the concept of "political incorporation" in that San Antonio has, in the last twenty years, elected a minority mayor, Henry Cisneros, who promised to use economic development strategies to solve poverty in those areas of the city where Latinos reside. This relationship, between having minority elected officials and how the economic development decisions are reached will provide additional evidence as to the biased nature of the capitalist state.

The only difficulty with using San Antonio to generalize about the general social and political conditions of Latinos in the United States is one of scope. The Latino community of San Antonio is unique in that it is the majority population in the city, possesses a large and active middle class, and has a lower percentage of immigrants from Latin America than any city of its type in the United States. San Antonio is approximately 56% Latino of whom 89% are of Mexican descent and 86% are citizens. There are large numbers of Mexican American professionals, lawyers, doctors, teachers, bureaucrats, businesspersons, and literati who participate in the daily life of the city. The social and political participation of Mexican Americans is so extensive in San Antonio that the culture itself is considered an important aspect of the city's environment. Spanish is spoken openly in the business and legal communities to the extent that it has become attractive for one to be bilingual in San Antonio. In all regards, the Latino community has become integrated, incorporated, into the daily political, social, and economic life of the city like no other in the United States. As a result, San Antonio, although unique among Latino cities, provides the "best case scenario" for evaluation of the incorporation of Latinos in the American political process. San Antonio, then, provides an excellent example to look at how the relationship between having minority politicians elected to office and how the economic development decisions that they are responsible for, substantively affect the Latino community. Methodologically, then, generalizing about the condition of all Latinos in the United States from San Antonio's situation is problematic in that one is on tenuous ground when generalizing from one case to a universe. However, the political and social uniqueness of San Antonio's Latino community provides an opportunity where one can observe how Latinos, under some of the most favorable conditions still fail to advance.

The data on electoral politics in San Antonio, Texas provides an in-depth look at how the Latino community has found it difficult to participate in the city's political life. Racial perceptions have found their way into the imaginations of San Antonio's electorate to the extent that they make their electoral decisions along racial lines. This results in racially polarized voting so intense that Latinos have been forced to sue the city under the Voting Rights Act of 1965 in order to have an opportunity to get elected to the city council. Still, the city has found that it can erect additional electoral barriers, such as instituting term limits, making it difficult for Latinos to continue participating politically.

Essentially, by using the social and political situation of Latinos in the liberal democratic state as the "data base" I will be able to test the proposition that the liberal democratic state bears a significant responsibility for creating and maintaining the unequal condition of Latinos in the United States. Additionally, this essay will provide grist for the perennial questions as to whether Latinos should pursue solely electoral gains as a way of alleviating their social and political inequality or whether some other approaches are more appropriate.

Some Definitional Clarifications

Earlier the terms "matrix" and "system" were used in reference to the state, however, it must be made clear that their use in this discussion is not intended to refer to the state in the same manner as utilized by Easton or those who espouse a "systems theory" approach to the study of the state. Rather, Whenever the term system is utilized it is intended to mean an arrangement, not necessarily orderly, of structures and processes that result in the ordering of the social relations of a society. I do not mean that the system has an output and input function that is continuous. I conceive of the state as having an unidentified number of channels through which the state interacts with its society and other states. In short, Easton's system is too rigid and not complex enough to represent the appropriate manner in which the state functions (1990).

When the term "matrix" is used throughout this discussion it is meant to represent a picture of the state as an arrangement of structures and processes organized in an infinitely complex manner. Although the structures and processes can be individually identified, they overlap or are part of each other and none are more important or come before another. Most importantly, some structures are essential aspects of each other. For instance, local political jurisdictions must consider legislative restrictions from the state and/or national level governments where appropriate in electoral and economic development policy arenas. Although the layers of government overlap and remain distinct, they also become institutionally integrated in the local decisional process.

The term "structure(s)" is used in the same manner in which both Foucault and Lyotard use it in that it is both an abstract and concrete phenomenon. In the former instance, abstract structures may include the very beliefs and belief systems that form the "glue" of a society. These beliefs are composed of structures that include and exclude various perceptions that fuel the direction of political action in activity often resulting in a specific public policy orientation. The rationale for the exclusion can be found in the notion that the appropriation of a private economic activity within a capitalist society is just not normally included as a viable policy option in one's training or in professional circles because it is not seen as a normal part of capitalist or liberal democratic thinking. Consequently, this type of policy alternative is automatically excluded from the range of all possible policy options during the decisional process. Instead, this type of option is supposed to be a normal topic of conversation in "command-type" economies or "communist-type" societies.

On a concrete level, structures represent the actual state apparatus such as a state or city government, a school district, or the office of the presidency. Generally, the state's structural parameters or jurisdictional limits are specifically identified in some law, constitution, charter, or ordinance. Although the parameter is institutionalized in the laws of a liberal democracy they reflect the principles of the ideology that dominates society, in this instance, liberal democratic society.

"Processes" should be understood as the manner in which decisions are reached within the state apparatus. These can include sets of rules or procedures, which guide decisional behavior, as well as the sets of norms and cultural values that guide the manner in which the various political actors interact with one another within the state or society.

At times I will refer to persons of Mexican national origin, who reside in the United States as Chicanos, Mexican Americans, or Latinos. My reference is not intended as an ideological statement but rather an attempt at overcoming redundancy in various passages of this work. To my friends from other Latin American countries who inquire as to the "nature" or origin of Mexican Americans I always counter with my perception that Chicanos are the northern-most Latin Americans in the Western Hemisphere being native to the United States. So we do have a separate identity in that we share aspects of United States

American culture but, on the other hand, we are Latinos. As a result I feel and I choose to identify as a Chicano, Mexican American, or Latino.

Outline of the Volume

Chapter One – The Theory of the Liberal Democratic State

The discussion in Chapter One will focus on the major arguments concerning the theory of the state that currently dominate the literature. The discussion will begin with an overview of the thinking that gave birth to the liberal democratic state beginning with Machiavelli and culminating with James Madison and other individuals who took part in the Constitutional Convention of 1787. This discussion is essential in that it is an attempt to trace the ideological principles that govern the contemporary state from their historical origins. By tracing the historical and ideological roots of the liberal democratic state one can obtain an understanding of why the state functions as it currently does.

Chapter Two – The Structural Barriers of the Liberal Democratic State

A structural analytical framework of the state is presented in this chapter. The discussion centers on Claus Offe's perception that the state is a filtering process that selects and excludes, from a broad range if policy preferences, those that are in the interests of the private sector. The economic development and judicial decisional structures are presented emphasizing the manner in which Latinos and their policy interests are systematically, structurally, eliminated from the public policy process. It is important to note that the elimination of Latinos and their interests from the policy process is not necessarily a conscious act but an act that is natural and normal to the policy process. This is so because the interests of out-groups such as Latinos, African Americans, the poor, and so forth are not supposed to be served by the liberal democratic state.

The rules governing participation in any state-sponsored activity such as economic development create an environment where only the business community as a whole may participate and all others are eliminated. Principally the private/public nexus causes this and is the defining keystone joining the state and the economy within a liberal democratic society. Once the state has legitimated the partnership, the private sector then provides the capital and material resources to conduct economic development activities wherever they wish, taking certain restrictions into mind of course. Many of these restrictions, such as environmental protection, building codes, interest rates, and so forth, are designed not to inhibit the private sector's performance but to protect the interests of the entire community. This allows the developmental process from becoming overly monopolistic and/or creating a threatening environment for other private sector investors. Latinos do not possess the resources to participate in either the public or private sector's economic developmental planning processes and therefore are not able to exert any or little influence over any decision that may significantly affect their community. The result is a decisional structure closed to the interests of Latinos but open to the interests of private sector investors.

Chapter Three – Chaos Theory and the Evolution of the State

Chapter Three's discussion will inventory Chaos or Nonlinear Dynamics Theory to uncover the principles that can be extrapolated and applied to the discussions on the theory of the state. The most important principles appear to be those that allow one to conceptualize of the state as a dynamical structure and whose form is dependent upon a broad array of variables or forces exerted from within and without the state system. These two principles, combined, explain why the state evolves over time and takes the particular form that it does.

Chapter Four – Social Inequality and the State Structure

The primary focus of this chapter is to explore the decisional structures and processes that determine the land use policies underlying the economic development decisions of San Antonio, Texas. The data presented in this chapter point out how the election of minority council members, including one of the most well educated and best prepared mayors in the city's history, did little to redirect the biased orientation of the city's economic development decisions. The reasons for the inability of the minority council-members to redirect the public policy process are many including their reliance on private sector support for election, the primacy of the public/private nexus, and the general assumptions underlying the decisions. Nevertheless, the resulting developmental decisions appear to do little to improve the general social conditions of the city's Mexican American community.

Additionally, this chapter reviews Latino political participation during the last thirty years of San Antonio's electoral history. Emphasis is placed on struggles the Mexican American community has undergone to obtain and maintain its ability to participate in the electoral and representative processes and structures of the city. Particular attention will be paid to the racially polarized nature of elections in San Antonio and the various barriers that have been placed and continue to be placed inhibiting the political participation of Mexican Americans. Some of these barriers have been overcome through the imposition of single member districts as a result of a Voting Rights law suit while others still remain to be overcome such as term limitations and city/county consolidation.

Chapter Five – A Dynamical Theory of the State and Latino Politics

The concluding chapter summarizes the major contributions of this volume and assesses them in light of the current arguments concerning the theory of the state and Latino Politics. Emphasis is placed on the principles generated by chaos theory concerning the essentiality of the state, how the state evolves throughout history, and why the state takes the form that it does within any historical era. Throughout the chapter the effects of the state on the United States Latino community are assessed. Finally, some implications for future research are discussed.

Chapter One

The Theory of the Liberal Democratic State

The essentiality of the state has been debated and discussed, intensely at times, since the dawning of the modern age of political theory (Carnoy, 1984). These discussions have ranged broadly covering topics ranging from what constitutes the conceptual foundation of the state to whether or not the state is autonomous and to what degree, to why the state takes the form it does, as well as to what causes the state to change form. In this chapter a brief review of selected literature in each of these areas will be presented in order to lay a foundation for the discussions in the remainder of the volume. Although not comprehensive, the review is intended to identify the major assumptions and perceptions of state theory in order to understand the principle arguments and concepts that have brought the theory to its current stage. The review also will develop an understanding of why the liberal democratic state structure takes the form it does.

The Nature of the State - The Classical Modern Thinkers
Niccolo Machiavelli

The state has been the central focus of political philosophy and theorists since the pre-Socratics; however, the modern era of political philosophy has traditionally been marked by the thoughts of Machiavelli. Many political scientists consider Niccolo Machiavelli the first of the modern political theorists for both his empirical approach to political analysis as well as being the first thinker, at least in the western tradition, to point out that the form of the state was subject to the rational machinations of individuals. Prior to Machiavelli, the

1

structural integrity of the state had never been questioned rather the state had been perceived as the ultimate authority in one's daily life. This perception was primarily the result of the relationship established between the Roman Catholic Church and feudal authorities. Although this almost theocratic relationship still reigned supreme during Machiavelli's lifetime, the corruption surrounding the Church's politics was beginning to draw the scrutiny of political observers. Machiavelli's observations, which appeared primarily in his <u>Discourses on the First Ten Books of Titus Livius</u> and <u>The Prince</u>, decried corrupt officials, both ecclesiastical and civil, as hindering the unity of Italy and the continuation of a stable state guided by men of *virtu.*[1] Machiavelli was not opting for some type of democracy on the contrary he was a firm believer of the need to have men of aristocratic background providing leadership for the state. What Machiavelli was concerned with primarily was pointing out to potential leaders the skills and virtues required in becoming efficient leaders. His strong Italian nationalism and his wish for a social stability that was lacking in a horribly fragmented Italian political world fueled Machiavelli's perception.

Machiavelli attempted to discern the rules that allowed the virtuous ruler to manipulate the state to achieve social stability. The genius of Machiavelli's work, however, laid in the fact that he pointed out that the virtuous ruler's actions would have two consequences. First, any political machination by the ruler inevitably resulted in some transformation of the state's form or structure. Additionally, the ruler's political judgment was always subject to the dictates of *fortuna.*[2] The end result was that virtuous rulers, although guided by virtue and morals, made decisions based on political practicalities. What was right was correct; what worked was the appropriate means to achieve a desired end.

In Machiavelli's perception, however, if the virtuous leader were able, together with his fellow citizens, to overcome corruption and the dictates of *fortuna*, then republican forms of government would arise. For Machiavelli this

---

[1] *Virtu*, for Machiavelli, is the intestinal fortitude and willingness of a leader to lead the state for the good of society generally.

was the most desirable form of the state. "His preference for popular government [was] not derived from any idea of individual 'rights,' but from the observation that popular governments are less cruel, unscrupulous, and inconsistent than tyrannous" (Russell, p. 509). Nevertheless, because times change, as does the course of human events, coupled with the fact that man is not always virtuous results in leaders and followers trying merely to survive daily. This results in wise or virtuous men ruling well during the times that they can control the forces of *fortuna* and despotically when they cannot. In this latter instance the leader, the Prince, must rely on his ability to manipulate the masses in order to become an effective ruler. Unfortunately, despotic governance is more common than good ones because virtuous leaders can only control *fortuna's* forces for a very short period of time. The key to the preservation of the state is that aristocratic and virtuous rulers must be extremely careful with the manipulative techniques they utilize in their attempts to preserve the state. If not, their control over the state becomes problematic and they may lose it.

Machiavelli, then, provided modern political thought with several very important conclusions concerning the modern state. First, the state is an artificial construct created by humans for self-protection and ruled by those who are the strongest and most able to provide the required protection. Secondly, the political actions of both rulers and followers can change the structural integrity of the state. Finally, because the ruler is continuously attempting to respond or react to the forces of *fortuna* the manner in which he responds can provide for the conditions resulting in the "degeneracy" of the state.

Thomas Hobbes

Strictly speaking, Thomas Hobbes produced work, which in terms of political philosophy marked the beginnings of the age of modernity. Hobbes's writings, principally _De Cive_ (1647) and _Leviathan_ (1651), reflect a concern over what type of state could protect society from the turmoil caused by the changing economic and social conditions of 17th Century Europe. In particular, Hobbes's

---

[2] *Fortuna* was seen as shaped by the interactions of men in responding to ever-present changes in human affairs. See Sibley (1970, p. 299).

two best known works were the culmination of his observations of the chaos rampant during the bloody Thirty Years War, a civil war between monarchists and parliamentarians, which raged in England between 1608-1648 resulting in the ascension to power of Oliver Cromwell.

Thomas Hobbes's observations were based on two assumptions that man possessed the ability to make a perfectly rational decision concerning the political world and that social chaos would exist if men were left to their own devices. Utilizing the metaphor of the state of nature where men exist side by side in a world with no institutions setting social guidelines, Hobbes rationalized that man relied upon his own abilities to do whatever was necessary for him to achieve self-preservation. This situation existed because all men were seeking to satisfy their own "appetites and aversions" and, consequently, would come into conflict with all other men. Hobbes concluded that this conflict resulted in a state of continuous civil war where life became "nasty, brutish, and short."

To overcome chaos and to rise above the "jungle" created by the conditions existing within a state of nature humans used their free will and reasoning capabilities to concoct a "social contract" with the remainder of society. Within this contract all men agreed to submit to the governance of a sovereign and supreme ruler who would, through any means at his disposal, insure social and political stability. Hobbes concluded that all political power must reside in the ruler for "covenants, without the sword, are but words." Some sort of governing institution was required to insure implementation of all laws that insured social stability. Essentially, Hobbes preferred a monarchy to a parliament or some type of assembly as the "Sovereign" who could bring order to a chaotic society efficiently and responsively. Thomas Hobbes simply felt that a monarchy provided clear and unidirectional leadership, efficiency of government, and quickness of response. Assemblies, in Hobbes's perception, were and are susceptible to division and, in the extreme case, civil war that was abhorrent. After all Hobbes had just seen thirty years of bloody civil war caused by the tension between a monarch and parliament.

Obviously, Hobbes admitted that sovereign governments could be susceptible to corruption and other despotic tendencies but this was preferable to anarchy and a small price to pay for social stability. Nonetheless, "the right of self-preservation he regards as absolute, and subjects [of the sovereign] have the right of self-defence...." Additionally, the subject does not have to submit to a sovereign if that ruler does not have the power to protect him (Russell, pp.552-3; Sibley, pp.350-52). In the final analysis, however, the sovereign could exercise whatever power he saw fit to insure social order.

Hobbes's contributions to the development of thought concerning the modern state were several. His notion of a social contract, although different from that which Locke and Rousseau would proffer, was unique in that it reiterated what Machiavelli had pointed out earlier; the power of the sovereign was based in the majority wishes of the populace. The power of the sovereign to provide for the security of his subjects, without any seeming constraints, also gave the state a sense of autonomy. Once the people had expressed their preference for a ruler they lost all rights except for those of self-preservation. The right of the people to "void" the contract, given the sovereign's inability to provide for the security of the population, was also unique. Unfortunately for Hobbes, however, he was living in the age of severe repression so he didn't expand on the notion or legitimacy of revolution. The principle issues emerging from Hobbes's works appear to be that the State was perceived as having centralized powers, an autonomous nature, found its legitimacy in the preferences of the people, and was responsible for managing conflict. Most importantly, however, was the notion that the state derived its legitimacy from the people and the people could, under certain circumstances, take that legitimacy away and shift it to a sovereign who could meet popular expectations.

The social stability resulting from the absolute nature of the sovereign was welcomed by the burgeoning commercial classes of Thomas Hobbes's day. Social stability, guaranteed by a strong state, would insure that the "new" emerging economic order would flourish and new wealth would be generated. However, the dual nature of the state, its absoluteness on one hand and its popular legitimacy on the other, bothered both monarchists and those preferring some type of democratic governmental arrangement. This seeming paradox provided the seed for the debates over liberal democracy that would dominate western society throughout the eighteenth century and give birth to the current modern state.

John Locke

Where Machiavelli and Hobbes provided the seeds for the discussions surrounding the creation of the modern state John Locke provided the first specific references to the types of political structures that would insure the stability of capitalism. The provision of individual liberties and the right to resist authority would become the theoretical lynchpins upon which Locke would begin his arguments (Sibley, p. 373). Locke is credited with being one of the guiding philosophers of the founders of the United States of America in that his concern with individual liberties, centricity of property rights, and right to resist despotic authorities appear throughout the Declaration of Independence and the Constitution of the United States. Needless to say, many constitutions of contemporary nations, presuming to be liberal democracies, also reflect the same Lockean concerns.

Locke's entire philosophical framework is based on the same empirical tradition pioneered by Hobbes. It is based upon observation (empiricism) and all human understanding came from observation and personal experience. Where Locke differed from Hobbes is in the notion that all men are initially rational so that rather than reacting to the "appetite and aversions" of man which make life so tenuous and dangerous in the state of nature, Locke's man sees respect for the lives of others.

"The *state of nature* (italics in the original) has a law of nature to govern it, which obliges every one: and reason, which is that law, teaches all mankind, who will consult it, that being all *equal and independent*, no one ought to harm another in his life, health, liberty, or possessions...." (Locke, p. 9).

So for Locke, as opposed to Hobbes, the state of nature is not necessarily a "jungle" but rather a world where all men are equal yet possess rationality to the point that it teaches man to respect the rights of others. Man does not seek to do everything he must to seek self-preservation but rather does what he must to preserve the state of nature insuring the equality and rights of others. Locke moved beyond what Hobbes could have possibly agreed with when later, in the same chapter of his Second Treatise on Civil Government, he states that man may even wish to lay down his life in order to preserve the state of nature. Locke reached this conclusion because he felt that all men were creatures and creations of God and that it was not within their rights to kill one another (Sibley, p. 377).

The concept central to Locke's perception of the state is that of the need to preserve one's property. Locke's notion of property is based in the belief that God gave the earth to be held in common by all men. At the same time God gave all men the ability to "subdue" the earth to provide, at least the industrious persons, wealth and material comforts (Locke, pp. 18-30). In the state of nature, however, man is willing to give up his liberty, which has allowed him to tame earth's resources, because the enjoyment of this right "is very uncertain, and constantly exposed to the invasion of others" (Locke, pp. 65-66). Although while in the state of nature all men are equal, "kings," as Locke puts it, and respect each other's property and possessions and the liberty to acquire such, "he is willing to quit a condition, which, however free, is full of fears and continual dangers...."(Locke, p. 66). In order for man to preserve his property, therefore, he must unite "into common-wealths, and putting themselves under government" (Locke, p. 66). This will allow for the creation of a set of "known laws" and provide for "indifferent judges" who will possess the power to execute the laws objectively (Locke, p. 66).

Locke was not particularly clear which type of state structure he preferred although he focused a great deal of attention on a type of representative governmental system. A representative type of system sprang from Locke's notion that whatever government would be imposed would be the result of some contractual arrangement among the population first and between the population and a sovereign government secondly.

In his Second Treatise of Government Locke points out that the most important power of government, whether placed in the hands of "one or many," is the legislative or law making power. This power to make laws cannot be used arbitrarily because the power was derived from all men in common and would also violate a basic law of nature. Keeping within the laws of nature, the legislative powers were to be "limited to the public good of society." Additionally, all laws formulated by the legislating powers must be known to all men and cannot be declared capriciously. Locke apparently preferred the public decisional processes to be open to scrutiny by the public in order to avoid any violations of the laws of nature or previously derived "standing rules." So that whoever were the arbitrators or implementers of the law were bound by the law that was supposed to prevent any ruler or ruling body from succumbing to the "appitites and aversions" (spelling in the original work) alluded to earlier by Hobbes. These laws, sanctioned by the populace, allowed for the objective dispensation of justice and resulted in the third governmental characteristic important to the Lockean scheme. The government was not allowed "to take from any man any part of his property without his consent: for the preservation of property being the end of government...."(Locke, p. 73).

Locke's ambivalence over whether a monarch or a representative form of government was the preferred structure may be a reflection of his political times. It is not clear whether England or Europe of the early eighteenth century was ready to accept a type of democracy that was only a philosophical proposal. What is certain is that John Locke's England and its fledgling colonies across the Atlantic were willing to allow discussion of this topic. As capitalism began to grow and flourish the discussions and debates over the specificity of an appropriate modern state would intensify throughout the remainder of the century.

The important contributions that Locke made to state theory were that he expanded the notion of a social contract from one where the population was willing to give up any rights to an absolute sovereign to one where the people invested law making and law giving responsibilities in a representative of their choice. Locke also pointed out the necessity of having a ruler or ruling entity that was responsible to the people for their rights. This linkage between the state's power and decisional capabilities and the people's material fortunes was an original conception in that prior to Locke the material well being of a citizenry was dependent upon the absolute actions and knowledge of the state. What Locke was implying was that the material well being of the populace was the responsibility of the people and the state was responsible for maintaining the political and legal conditions which would allow for the people to continually enjoy material good fortune. If the state failed to provide this stability, through the usurpation of authority or by the ceding of authority to another, then political power reverts to the people who then must decide what new form of government to create or to select someone else to legislate for them (Locke, pp. 102-24).

So, then, one sees the emergence in the writings of John Locke of one of the foremost principles of liberal democracy--the notion that government must be limited and it should not interfere in the world of private property. Consequently, the preferred liberal democratic government was one that insured social stability so that the pursuit of material well being could continue unfettered and with a minimal amount of political fear or apprehension poisoning the social environment. One of Locke's oversights, although it may not have been, given his social status, was that material well being is uneven in society and that the pursuit of this well being laid in the hands of a privileged few (Sibley, p. 385). Latter thinkers such as Jeremy Bentham, John Stuart Mill, and Adam Smith would expand upon these liberal democratic principles while the social oversight would be the subject of Jean Jacques Rousseau.

Jean Jacques Rousseau

Political thinkers prior to Rousseau spoke of the state as an abstraction lacking both specificity and a definite linkage to social and political reality. Machiavelli, Hobbes, and Locke understood that social inequality existed and that the inequality could lead to political chaos. However, each thought that the inequality was a natural consequence of birth or fortune and that the resulting unrest, civil war or chaos, was justification for state absolutism. Jean Jacques Rousseau, on the other hand, clearly provided the perspective that would expand the analysis of the relationship between the modern state and social reality. Rousseau's work appears to provide the conceptual bridge between the classical modern thinkers, represented here by Machiavelli, Hobbes, and Locke, and those who wrote specifically about liberal democracy.

The state, in Rousseau's perception, was supposed to intervene not after the occurrence of political chaos but before. Rousseau felt that "There will always be a vast difference between subduing a mob and governing a social group" (Rousseau, 1762, p. 178). He concluded that if inequality, resulting from the unfettered pursuit of material gain, were minimized then chaos would not arise. The state's responsibility was to insure that a minimal of material inequality resulted from the accumulation of "real property."

Rousseau's contributions to the theory of the state discussions began with the notion that in a state of nature man was without morality, capable of evil, and corrupted by the ownership of property. For Rousseau, property was a source of evil and inequality, the formation of civil society was the product of man's greed because it was the work of the wealthy and socially powerful, society was formed in the interests of the wealthy and not for the benefit of the masses. An unequal society required the preservation of order to prevent any attempts at the disruption of the social status quo and to legitimize the exploitation of the poor. In Rousseau's perception, unlike previous thinkers, it was impossible to separate social and political inequality (Carnoy, p. 21). Therefore, the liberal democratic state had to be an interventionist state in order to preserve the interests of the rich and powerful and to keep the masses under control.

Rousseau's reliance on the state of nature to begin his analysis reflects both a popular analytical starting point and a manner in which to begin a logical and objective discussion on why and how one can make a political decision. The state of nature was a popular starting point because any and all persons who wished to participate in the political theorizing of the 17th and 18th century appeared to begin their analysis with this paradigm. On the other hand, the state of nature was a rather "nifty" device that would allow one to begin an analysis with a minimal number of presuppositions or assumptions. In other words, it was an attempt at creating an analytical "*tabula rasa*" from which to begin a political discourse. Rousseau, however, understood this in that he felt that the state of nature did not exist, probably never or would exist "and of which nonetheless it is necessary to have just ideas, in order to judge well our present state" (Rousseau, 1754).

The use of the state of nature in his analytical framework was required, according to Rousseau, so that natural law(s) could be deduced. Without this deduction man could not determine the laws best suited to his state, the general will could not, therefore, be determined, and civil society could not exist (Russell, p. 688). For Rousseau, however, the state of nature is one where there are no laws other than whatever an individual can concoct in his own mind and exercise with his own physical abilities. Rousseau felt that the exercise of physical strength to get one's way was without moral sanction, that "to yield to the strong is an act of necessity, not of will. At most it is the result of a dictate of prudence" (Rousseau, 1762, p. 172). As long as "might made right" the resulting social relationship between individuals would always be of "master and Slave, never of People and Ruler. .... It implies neither public welfare nor a body politic" (Rousseau, 1762, p. 178). What was needed to make the movement from a state of nature to a civil society was a state and this could only evolve through the creation of a General Will.

The General Will was the reflection of the social contract that all members of society entered into. This agreement would enable them to "develop some sort of central direction and learn to act in concert" (Rousseau, 1762, p. 179). The

11

Social Contract would allow for "some form of association" which would result in enlisting the whole strength of the community "for the protection of the person and property of each constituent member, in such a way that each, when united to his fellows, renders obedience to his own will, and remains as free as he was before" (Rousseau, 1762, p. 180). The Contract had to be understood by all members of society so that they would make a perfect union, all would submit because all would understand and agree to the "clauses in question." All must surrender their rights to all other members of society, the surrendering of rights would make all equal socially and politically. This surrendering he called "the act of association." Rousseau concluded that

> As soon as the act of association becomes a reality, it substitutes for the person of each of the contracting parties a moral and collective body made up of as many members as the constituting assembly has votes, which body receives from this very act of constitution its unity, its dispersed *self*, and its will (1762, p. 180)

This joining together, this association produced the "Public Person" or the State, each member was known as a Citizen because they shared in the sovereign authority and as a Subject because they owed obedience to the laws of the State. The laws of the State, in turn, were a reflection of the General Will. The movement from a state of nature to the "civil state," therefore, results in the substitution of "justice" for "instinct" and gives a moral basis for political and social decisions.

Rousseau felt that the General Will conferred on all the benefits of citizenship to include what he called "Moral Freedom." This would allow an individual to overcome what Hobbes called "appetites and aversions" and result in achieving freedom through the obedience to the laws promulgated by society. These laws were primarily designed to prevent the social chaos caused by the temptations surrounding the acquisition of material wealth that to Rousseau translated into property. Rousseau felt that the "real founder of civil society" was the "first man who ... enclosed a piece of land" (1754, p. 207). He felt that the real foundation of civil society was the ownership of property but that if extremes in ownership resulted then the State would be threatened. Rousseau felt that all men were equal "in the eyes of the law" and the state's responsibility was to insure this equality. In an interesting footnote to his Social Contract Rousseau pointed out that

> Under a bad government such equality is but apparent and illusory. It serves only to keep the poor man confined within the limits of his poverty, and to maintain the rich in their usurpation. In fact, laws are always beneficial to the 'haves' and injurious to the 'have-notes.' Whence it follows that life in a social community can thrive only when all its citizens have something, and none have too much. (1762, p. 189).

Rousseau's observation appeared as a warning, a harbinger to the dangers in an unfettered market society. According to C. B. MacPherson, Rousseau saw property as the means of producing life and that "private property is a sacred individual right" (MacPherson, 1977, p. 16). However, Rousseau felt that "a man must occupy only the amount [of land] he needs for his subsistence" (1762, p. 187). Rousseau concluded that the ownership of limited amounts of property was a reflection of the General Will and was necessary to the prevention of social inequality because "no citizen shall ever be wealthy enough to buy another, and poor enough to be forced to sell himself" (1762, p. 217). In other words some wealth was fine; too much wealth was a threat to freedom. Therefore, Rousseau saw material inequality as a violation of the General Will that would eventually lead to the creation of a society divided along class lines. The state that Rousseau proposed, then was one that had as its "most important functions ... to prevent extreme inequality of fortunes; not by taking wealth from its possessors, but by depriving all men of means to accumulate it; not by building hospitals for the poor, but by securing the citizens from being poor" (1758, p. 267). For Rousseau the key to having a "solid and enduring State" is to have a society without material extremes; it must be a society having neither "millionaires nor beggars". These are inseparable from one another, and both are fatal to the common good. One produces the makers of tyrants, the other, tyrants themselves. Where they exist, public liberty becomes a commodity to barter. The rich buy it, the poor sell it" (1762, p. 217).

Having linked the social welfare of a society to the accumulation of wealth process and placing the responsibility of moderating or managing this process in the hands of the state, all that remained for Rousseau was to specify which state structure or set of institutional arrangements were appropriate to the task. In Book III of his Social Contract Rousseau defined what he felt was meant by "government." Government was supposed to be a "body" which fostered communications between "subjects" and "sovereigns" "and it is charged with the execution of the laws and the maintenance of liberty, both civil and political" (Rousseau, p. 222).

Rousseau felt that the legislative power, the law-making power, resided in the hands of the people and he was very clear that they could never abrogate the legislative power or it could lead to "despotism or anarchy." The executive power, on the other hand, remained in the hands of the sovereign who was responsible for executing the laws and protecting the legislated liberties of the people. Rousseau pointed out that a delicate balance had to be maintained between the executive and legislative powers, between the sovereign and the people. This balance was the key to the State's longevity and survival because "a thousand different events may change the balance within a nation" (Rousseau, p. 223). In the same passage Rousseau pointed out, as he did in an earlier book of the Social Contract, that the government's structure should be suited also to the peculiarities of a given society. Additionally, a government's form may be different from time to time given political and civil exigencies.

It appears, then, that the most significant contributions made by Rousseau in regards to the manner in which the modern state can be perceived include the notion that the structure should possess several branches particularly separating the legislative from the executive powers; that the state's form may take on differing structures from one society to another; that a government's form may change from one historical era to another; and, that embedded within the state are the seeds of its own demise or continued existence. These last two notions are of particular concern in that they indicate that Rousseau assumed the state to be a continually changing entity, that the state, on an abstract level, can be conceptualized as a fluid entity rather than as a static construct. This notion separated Rousseau from all previous western political thinkers.

For Rousseau the demise of the state could come about because of the erosion of the delicate balance that needed to exist between the legislative and executive bodies. Without the legitimacy of the legislative powers, always residing with the people, the executive would erode. If the executive usurped the legislating powers of the subjects then the liberties of the people would be threatened. In the first instance this type of imbalance would lead to anarchy and in the second it would lead to despotism. Rousseau felt that

> The body politic, no less than the body human, begins to die from
> the very moment of its birth, and carries within itself the causes of
> its own destruction. ....they [man] can prolong the life of the
> State for as long as possible by devising for it the best conceivable
> form. (Rousseau, p.254)

He then goes on to state that the

> The principle of political life is in the sovereign authority. The
> Legislative Power is the heart of the State, the Executive is its

> brain, and gives movement to all its parts. The brain may be struct
> by paralysis and the patient yet live. .... But once the heart ceases
> to function, it is all over with the animal (Rousseau, p. 254).

So then in order for the state to survive it must maintain the balance between the legislative and executive. Most importantly, however, the legislative power must remain in the hands of the people or the state will die.

Rousseau felt, however, that the disruption of the delicate balance between the legislative and executive powers was not the only threat to the state. The machinations of other states (Rousseau, p. 215) can also become a threat to the state's existence. The maintenance of the state's internal stability is the key to the continuing existence of the state in light of both external and internal threats. Rousseau, although he did not explicitly state this, appears to have left room for the notion that, because states can pass from existence and because they must continuously act to counter any internal or external threats, states always change form. In other words the actions or measures the state takes to prevent its demise or to ward off external or internal threats inevitably results in some change to the state's structure and, consequently, its form. Thus, although it appears that the state is threatened with extinction it is really placed in a situation where, in order to counter extinction, it will modify its structures through the passage and implementation of laws and the creation of agencies to manage any threats to its integrity (Rousseau, p. 223). So, simply put, almost any action on the part of the state causes structural changes within the state. Finally, these state machinations appear as the result of changes fostered by changing internal or external social relations.

The Nature of the State - The Liberal Democratic Thinkers
Adam Smith

16

Traditional political science often overlooks the contributions to the theory of the state made by Adam Smith. Principally, Adam Smith is viewed as an economist and the "Father of Capitalism." However, in The Theory of Moral Sentiment (1759) and The Wealth of Nations (1776), Smith set forth both his economic theories and his perception of the type of state that would be compatible with such a system.

Adam Smith based many of his economic and political perceptions on the *laissez-faire* assumption popularized by the French economist François Quesnay in his *Tableau Economique* (1758). Quesnay felt that since the state was an artificial construct it should not interfere, or at least as little as possible, in the natural world. Since wealth is derived from the soil it is a natural consequence of how man interacts with nature, naturally. If the state stays out of the economic world then it will rule "physiocratically" and man will achieve natural harmony not an artificially contrived, state induced harmony. The least state intervention, the more naturally harmonious society becomes. Mulford Q. Sibley also points out that this physiocratic school of thought probably had a great deal of influence on Thomas Jefferson's thinking (p. 388).

Nevertheless, the *lassez-faire* school of thought predominated the methodology used by Adam Smith in reaching his conclusions concerning capitalism and the type of state required for the smooth functioning of the "new" economic order. Smith assumed that underlying all social relations was a compassion for the well being of others and society generally. Smith also felt that the best interests, the overall economic health of society, could best be served through the natural pursuit of wealth. The generation of wealth would produce both riches for the wealthy and work (labour) for the working segments of society. There was a slight "glitch," however, in that there are always those among both rich and poor, who will, because of envy or necessity, disrupt the accumulation process.

17

> But avarice and ambition in the rich, in the poor the hatred of
> labour and the love of present ease and enjoyment, are the passions
> which prompt to invade   property.... (Smith, [1776]   1937,
> p. 670)

The "invasion of property" was directly attributable to the extremes of material
inequality that Smith foresaw as an integral consequence of capitalism.

> Wherever there is great property, there is great inequality. For one
> very rich man, there must be at least five hundred poor, and the
> affluence of the few supposes the indigence of the many. (Smith,
> [1776] 1937, p. 670)

The extreme material differences have dual effects on society. The poor become
resentful and envious of the lifestyles and material wealth of the rich while the
rich become fearful of losing their wealth to the poor. This class tension gives
rise to the necessity of the state.

> The affluence of the rich exites the indignation of the poor, who
> are both driven by want, and prompted by envy, to invade his [the
> wealthy] possessions. It is only under the shelter of the civil
> magistrate that the owner of that valuable property... can sleep a
> single night in security. He is at all times surrounded by unknown
> enemies, whom, though he never provoked, he can never appease,
> and from whose injustice he can be protected only by a powerful
> arm of the civil magestrate.... The acquisition of valuable and
> extensive property, therefore, necessarily requires the
> establishment of civil government. (Smith, [1776] 1937, p. 670)

18

Adam Smith felt that although the pursuit and acquisition of wealth was eventually going to result in the betterment of society, the accumulation process would result in unintended inequalities that could cause ill feelings among both competitors and the working classes. The infringement of private property (material wealth), in Adam Smith's perception, was seen as unjust because the only manner in which to properly accumulate wealth was through "the labour of many years, or perhaps of many successive generations" (Smith, [1776] 1937, p. 670).

Smith, however, viewed the state less favorably then he did the private sector. He felt that the state was susceptible to "public prodigality and misconduct." Additionally, he felt that "the whole public revenue, is in most countries employed in maintaining unproductive hands" ([1776] 1937, p. 325). Smith was not speaking to those on the public dole but to almost everyone employed by the government including

> "the people who compose a numerous and splendid court, a great ecclesiastical establishment, great fleets and armies, who in time of peace produce nothing, and in time of war acquire nothing which can compensate the expence of maintaining them, even while the war lasts. Such people, as they themselves produce nothing, are all maintained by the produce of other men's labour." ([1776] 1937, p. 325)

Public employment, particularly undue public employment, consumed resources required for the accumulation process, which fueled the health of capitalism. The key to social stability, apparently, was to strike a balance between the necessity of having an interventionist government or state and how far to allow the state or government to intervene.

Smith's political economy, then, called for the primacy of the free market and the subordination of a minimally sized state apparatus. He saw that the individual pursuit of wealth, when aggregated translated into the collective well being of society. The end result, the real goal if you will, of a free market economy is the collective well being of society. The role of the state was to protect the interests and activities of those who were pursuing the generation of individual wealth, which would lead to the overall well being of society. This protection of the interests of the wealthy and well to do from the usurpatious appetites of the poor and envious was Adam Smith's definition of justice and the only authentic role for the state or "civil magistrates."

Adam Smith's contributions to liberal democratic thought were to provide the economic argument for the existence of a state (Marxists are accused of being economic determinists but it appears that the father of capitalism, writing before Marx, was guilty of this manner of thinking first). Smith also created the perception that appears unchanged to this day that public sector expenditures are nonproductive. Additionally he for provided the rationale, rightly or wrongly, of the primacy of markets over the state and for setting forth the relationship between the structure and superstructure--"that is, the relation between production (the invisible hand) and the cohesive forces that bind society" (Carnoy, p. 29). Adam Smith also highlighted the notion that a capitalist society must, by definition, be a society where classes and material inequalities exist and flourish. Finally, Smith pointed out that a class based society is one where tensions between the classes will arise and can lead to social anarchy or disruption if the state does not maintain control over that tension.

The Utilitarians - Jeremy Bentham, James Mill, and John Stuart Mill

Like Adam Smith, Bentham and both Mills were intellectual descendants of David Hume who many consider the founder of modern empiricism and the first leading expounder of utilitarianism. Jeremy Bentham, as did Smith and James and John Stuart Mill, nevertheless, appeared to derive their notion of the state not as the principal institution in their world view but as an institution that would complement what they defined as the primary function of all humans--the pursuit of security and happiness through the production and accumulation of wealth.

It appears that most of the liberal democratic thinkers whose works gave birth to the modern state concentrated on describing the assumptions and motivations driving man's pursuit of subsistence within society. All of these writers produced their works between the middle of the seventeenth through the first third of the nineteenth centuries. The earlier writers, represented here by Hobbes, Locke, and Rousseau, exemplified the writing of what has come to be known as the Enlightenment Period. This historical era featured the first attempts at depicting man's behavior as the result of a rationalization process based upon some identified fundamental needs. These needs whether described as resulting from "appetites or aversions," as Hobbes put it, had one goal in common, the pursuit of wealth to insure one's long term security.

Sheldon Wolin, however, poignantly pointed out that the political philosophers of the Enlightenment Era were struggling with the construction of a new world view given the quick evolution of a dramatically new way of viewing the world economically. Essentially, Adam Smith's capitalism featured seemingly unlimited opportunities for the acquisition of wealth assuming the limitlessness of the world's natural resources, advancing technological innovations, and the desire and industriousness of his modern man. Underlying this wondrous new economic world, however, was an anxiety created by Thomas Robert Malthus with his popular theory of overpopulation. Essentially, Malthus's pronouncements underscored the notion that eventually there would come a time when a dearth of resources would have to be confronted (1798). Smith, Locke, Bentham recognized this, and, particularly, James Mill. Wolin suspects that the "happiness principle," which was the utilitarian goal, was really the reverse side of a "pain principle." Wolin suggests that man made decisions seeking happiness out of fear that if they did not pursue specific avenues to their fullest then they would experience pain. Man's daily existence, then, was a constant struggle waged against other struggling men. Hobbes likened this social situation to a "nasty, brutish, jungle." Consequently, Wolin concludes that "the anxieties besetting liberal man were rooted in his belief in the ever-present possibility of pain and that this belief, in turn, shaped in an important way his attitudes toward the role of government, the possibilities of political action, the nature of justice, and the function of law and legal penalties." (p. 326).

So then one of the motivating factors for many of the liberal democratic writers was the fear of political and social chaos that pervaded their times. Not only were nation states being born but also feudal society and mercantilism were quickly passing from the historical stage. Mercantilism was evolving into industrial capitalism spurred on by a veritable explosion of technological innovations (Boorstin, 1985). Feudalism, on the other hand, was experiencing change as well, however, exactly what feudalism, as a political system, was changing into was not clear. So that modern, liberal writers such as Adam Smith, Jeremy Bentham, and James and John Stuart Mill concentrated most of their writings on rationalizing the legitimacy of the economic order as the result of nature's ordering. As Wolin points out, however, their rationalization was constructed in an extremely "cunning" manner and "happiness was tracked down methodically precisely because of the scarce nature of the objects with which it can be identified." (p. 325). Essentially, Smith, Bentham, and the Mills painted a rosy picture of an economic order that justified the accumulation of material goods and wealth in a 17th and 18th Century world of scarce resources and goods.

Liberal thinkers assumed that the pursuit of happiness and wealth, which were and are still equated, would inevitably lead to unequal social conditions because of the natural inequality of man and the eventual scarcity of resources. They assumed that all men, although equal as species beings, were unequal as far as natural abilities and degrees of industriousness were concerned. The inequality among men would translate into unequal material and social conditions within society. All agreed that material inequalities would lead to an insecure society that, in turn, would result in a "pushing and pulling contest" (Locke) or "an unusual scramble" (Bentham) among different types of ruling groups for money,

22

power, and prestige (Wolin, p. 325). Essentially, liberal thinkers knew that the social inequality engendered by capitalism could lead to social strife and violence. This liberal anxiety, as Wolin aptly describes the intellectual atmosphere of that era, led liberal thinkers to turn to a yet unborn modern state to insure much needed and wished for security.

Although the feudal state existed, its structure and the manner in which it reached public policy decisions, it tended toward absolutism, were not appropriate to the goals of industrial capitalism. What was needed was a state apparatus that could both provide the political and legal security required by the free markets of that era and, at the same time, not prove to be a state that would interfere in any market machinations. Essentially, the state was supposed to maintain control over society generally and the laborers specifically in order to provide safety for those in pursuit of material gain. Nevertheless, liberal thinkers found themselves in a quandary in that they saw government as a necessary evil that was unproductive economically. Not only was any government economically unproductive the only method of financing such an entity was through some sort of taxation scheme paid for by the captains of capitalism. Bentham saw that "production depended on investment, and hence the decision as to where and how capital ought to be invested was always governed by the fixed amount of capital available" (Wolin, p. 319). So then the "fundamental principle of 'groundwork of the whole' was 'the limitation of industry by the limitation of capital'. It was this proposition that dictated the classical attack on all forms of government interference. Bounties, monopolies, preferential taxation, etc., were all based on the fallacy that new wealth could be produced by government regulation" (Bentham cited in Wolin, p. 319). It appears that this late eighteenth century perception of government has remained relatively unchanged in the late twentieth century. Currently, those who argue against government taxation stipulate that taxes remove much needed capital from the hands of investors thereby inhibiting growth potential. Minimal or no taxation allows investors to pursue developmental activities that will provide more social goods than the government can possibly provide. This is true because the private sector argues that their investments produce goods, create jobs, and generate conditions for additional investment opportunities. The state, on the other hand, can provide nothing useful except the physical security required insuring a stable social system.

The Liberal Democratic State in the United States

Although government was viewed as wasteful and unproductive by liberal thinkers, they did feel that the government was necessary to provide a certain degree of social control. These critics of government, however, did not wish to have the population totally subjugated, to do so would be to alienate the working classes and, in the end, to destabilize the accumulation process. So, then, the liberal state envisioned by Bentham, whatever its structure, would guarantee the best distribution of rights and obligations, the best set of laws which would produce the greatest happiness of the greatest number (Macpherson, 1977, p. 27). The State had to nurture Adam Smith's free market system and protect citizens from corrupt and rapacious government. As an extension, elections and freedom of the press were essential. These two institutions allowed the people to keep politicians in check (Carnoy, p. 30). John Stuart Mill, although feeling that extending political participation broadly was a desirous end because of its efficacious value, did not trust the perception or decision making capabilities of the working class. This dilemma also perplexed the framers of the United States Constitution. Mill's solution to this paradox was to champion some type of representative governmental arrangement that would both mathematically and institutionally dilute the voice of the working classes and the poor.

The state envisioned by liberal thinkers as compatible with and dependent upon capitalism would then appear to feature the following characteristics. There had to be some sort of executive institution that would be responsible for administering the state on a daily basis. The law making powers, however, were never to be abrogated by the people but placed in the hands of some representational body. The representational body was to be elected from a set of identified electors. Since all liberal thinkers understood that their society was

24

composed of unequal classes of persons it would be logical to conclude that the franchise was to be awarded to those understanding and having an interest in insuring that the market remained the principle institution of society. The composers of the United States Constitution, which gave birth to the first modern liberal democratic state in Western Civilization, defined the franchise qualifications by allowing only those males owning property to vote. Elections also had to occur regularly so that those representing the people were always felt to be beholding to their constituents. An additional check on members of the executive and legislative bodies was the existence of a free press. A "free press" that was free from the state's control but an essential member of the business community so not free from commercial control.

The state's powers would be limited to doing what it deemed necessary to insure that the free market operated as freely as possible. This included protecting market activity from both internal and external threats. Protecting the market was to be the primary reason for the state's existence. Since the market provided the wealth undergirding a society's social stability and standard of living it behooved the government to do everything possible to insure the market's security. An unsecured market would fall victim to both internal and external threats and result in the possible political destabilization of the working classes or, at least, a society's ability to maintain control over the working classes.

The threat to the market place's security lay in the state's ability to achieve and maintain the delicate balance between the powers of the sovereign (executive) and the people (legislative). Maintenance of the delicate balance would insure that the executive would not usurp its powers and either become overly involved in or neglect the security of the market. All liberal thinkers felt that some understanding between the executive and legislative bodies was required and that any executive who usurped the office's powers was not worthy of the people's support. Early thinkers, however, such as Machiavelli, Hobbes, Locke, and Rousseau did not or would not champion the overthrow of the executive. So it was never quite clear as to what the people should do given an unresponsive executive. The later liberal thinkers, on the other hand, solved this dilemma by championing some sort of electoral mechanism whereby voters or electors could periodically replace members of the executive. The complication with this system was the general distrust, on the part of the thinkers, for the decision-making capabilities of the working classes given their lack of education and their small stake in the market. After all, the working classes only benefited in a very limited manner from the investment decisions of capitalists. Additionally, the governmental apparatus had to be responsive to society's economic leaders because their market decisions would provide for the long-term economic and social well being of that society. It appears that this was the principle rationale for limiting the franchise to only those owning property in the United States of the eighteenth century. Finally, because the scope of governmental influence was limited so, it would seem, would the size of government.

The framers of the *United States Constitution*, as substantiated by many of the *Federalist Papers*, based the parameters of the new government on the principles derived from liberal thinkers. Charles Beard's classical work, <u>An Economic Interpretation of the Constitution of the United States</u> (1913), underscores the intentions of the framers as they created the structure of the national government. The principle intent was to create a governmental system, which would protect the economic interests of the new country internationally and domestically by insuring that the new system could manage and control any external or internal forces that may threaten the "new" country's social stability. These interests were not necessarily specific, although Beard does point out rather clearly that those who participated in the Constitutional Convention would gain materially from the creation of a government that guaranteed payment on the huge debt the government had incurred during and prior to the Revolutionary War.

The new government, nevertheless, was designed to do more than just protect the narrow interests of a few individuals. The new government also was designed to insure a stable social setting within which capitalism would thrive both inside the jurisdictional boundaries of the new country and in an extremely conflict ridden world economy. Beard contends that the latter reason is the basis for the special emphasis on the founding of an army and navy in the new constitution. He substantiates his position with Alexander Hamilton's perception that the "real sources of conflict (internecine warfare)" is commercial conflict (The Federalist, No. 3). In the very next essay, The Federalist No. 4, Hamilton extends his analysis from the international realm to the domestic by pointing out that the new constitution will go far in arbitrating disputes between states over commerce and geographical interests, the regulation of public debt, and the protection of contractual rights. The only mechanism that could provide for the requisite stability was a "firm union" that reflected the general interests of its population.

It is clear from The Federalist, particularly Nos. 9 and 10 penned by Hamilton and James Madison respectively, that the principle function of government was as "a barrier against domestic faction and insurrection"(p. 47) and "its tendency to break and control the violence of faction"(p. 53). In Madison's perception, the "most common and durable source of factions has been the various and unequal distribution of property. Those who hold and those who are without property have ever formed distinct interests in society. .... The regulation of these various and interfering interests forms the principal task of modern legislation, and involves the spirit of party and faction in the necessary and ordinary operations of government" (The Federalist, No. 10, p. 56).

The fear of factions and social discontent, the latter of which was exemplified by Shays' Rebellion and the talk of a military coupe, was reflected in much of the correspondence between many of the Constitutional Convention participants (Beard, The Rise of Civilization, p. 307, passim and Zinn, A People's History of the United States, pp. 90-95).[3] This fear, of almost paranoiac proportions, was the same fear reflected in the writings of the liberal democratic and capitalist thinkers who dominated the ideological dialogue of the 18th

---

[3] Charles Beard discusses these perceptions, citing Farrand's classical "Report of the American Historical Association, 1903" on certain compromises of the Constitution throughout Chapter III of An Economic Interpretation of the Constitution of the United States.

Century. Adam Smith, James Mill, John Locke, and Jean Jacques Rousseau understood quite well that the new economic order would "naturally" create social and economic inequalities. Other thinkers, James Madison was numbered among this group, felt that the inequalities were due to the "diversity in the faculties of men." Another group, whose thinking is represented by Adam Smith, felt that inequalities could arise by the unfettered greed of unscrupulous individuals who manipulated the market to their advantage. While still others felt, Rousseau is representative of this perception, that the inheritability of wealth would feed the inequality inherent to capitalism.

Economic inequality would lead to social inequality and the general inequality would lead to jealousy, frustration, and anger among the poor. Eventually this social discontent would create violent situations that would threaten the ability of the wealthy to accumulate capital. Smith or his contemporaries did not write about full-blown theories of revolution but the fear of "sleeping safely in one's bed" was mentioned as an artifact of the envy and anger of the poor.

The "Biased" New Liberal Democratic State

The fear of the propertyless eventually found its way into the thinking surrounding the construction of the new government. Many of the framers were afraid that those without property, which were also those without legal standing and/or education, would gain some foothold in the new political processes and elect some of their own kind to office. This bias against the less educated participating in United States politics has been reflected in the history of how the franchise has been reluctantly extended to members of various racial minority groups and women. The fear to extend the franchise is based on the fear that these "out groups" do not share the same general interests as the "in groups." The fear is that the elected representatives of these disfranchised groups could pass legislation that would affect deleteriously the institutional parameters required for the smooth operation of a capitalist economic system. This, in turn, could threaten the hegemonic position of the wealthy in a capitalist society.

The key to how the new government was to be structured lay in how both Hamilton and Madison perceived the role of government and the paranoia expressed by many of the framers. The "best" governmental or state structure was one that could moderate any conflicts that arose from the ill distribution of wealth within society. Although, this unequal distribution was a "normal" consequence of capitalism, in itself, it was not perceived as something "bad." Social inequality has existed historically throughout the history of western civilization and reflected in the writings of almost every political thinker within this tradition. Social inequality was deemed normal and/or natural and to be tolerated but not necessarily to be eradicated. Without social inequality there would be no class of workers to do the manual productive, menial labor, or the distasteful work of society. The principle function, however, of the modern state was how to manage the inequality so as to prevent conflict from arising that would threaten the very structure of that society.

Beard's review of the sentiments of each of the participants in the Constitutional Convention provides glimpses of what the new governmental structure would eventually become. With only two exceptions, Nathanial Gorham and Luther Martin, every member of the convention looked suspiciously at the possibility of granting the franchise to anyone who was not a "freeholder," in other words a property holder. The basic assumption was that the ownership of property gave the individual a vested interest in insuring that the existing economic system was to be nurtured so that its growth would go uninhibited and progress naturally. Although a property qualification does not appear in the Constitution, Beard points out that the primary reason this is so is because the franchise was determined and administered by state laws and agencies. Clinton Rossiter pointed out that all states with the exception of Vermont granted the franchise only to tax payers and those who held property (The Political Thought of the American Revolution, pp. 191-92). It is clear, then, that only those free males who owned property were allowed to vote in Federal elections. Women were not granted the franchise; African Americans were still, for the most part, slaves;

29

Native Americans were considered members of some alien race and/or nation; and Latinos did not even exist as they do today. As a matter of fact the United States Government did not recognize Latinos as a social or political category until 1930 and then the Census Bureau listed them as "Mexicans". The Mexican category and any other reference to other Latinos was dropped by the Bureau until 1960 and has been continuously changed every census enumeration period since. Generally Latinos have enjoyed an ambivalent existence as far as the United States Government is concerned being included in "White" and "Black" categories and subdivided among a broad array of ethnic groups (Goldberg, 1997). Naturally all of these groups were excluded from participating in the political system and processes of the new nation either consciously or unconsciously.

An interesting aside, having implications for certain aspects of current debates over the legitimacy and viability of the Voting Rights Act, the franchise and representation were treated as two unrelated issues. When the debate over how to count slaves as far as representation was concerned they were included in the apportionment process in order to give southern states such as South Carolina a numerical foundation that would allow for higher numbers of representatives to be allotted in the United States House of Representatives. One of the "constitutional compromises" was to count the slaves as three-fifths of a person for purposes of both representation and taxation. Still, slaves were not accorded the right to vote (Beard, The Rise of American Civilization, p. 319). So the framers' intent as to whether one needs to be a voter in order to be counted as part of the apportionment process was clear--representational apportionment was to be based on population rather than on the franchise count. The framers, however, did not wish or failed to connect the two issues for whatever reason. Currently, much to do is made concerning the need to only count citizens or registered voters when determining the size of a representational district as opposed to the general population or the voting age population. It appears that if the entire population was to be represented then it would be appropriate to use the general population numbers to determine the proper apportionment ratio. If, however, representation was intended to be limited to particular segments of the population then those relevant population figures should be used in the calculations.

Nevertheless, how the national assembly was to be constructed and who was to sit in the appropriate chamber was a matter of much discussion. Some of the framers felt that a unicameral structure was appropriate while others felt two chambers were essential to maintaining a check on the other house. Since office holding and the franchise were restricted to property holders this did not become an issue. The requirement for two chambers, however, appears to have been based upon a social class requisite. The framers felt that those of lesser property should be represented in one chamber while those of wealthier classes should have their chamber. Initially, property qualifications were set forth for membership in each chamber with Charles Pinckney actually wanting to stipulate a specific value amount for the holding of all offices including the Executive and Judiciary (Beard, p. 211). The convention members finally settled on two chambers where the membership of one was elected by property holders, the House of Representatives, and apportioned by the population while membership in the other was limited to those selected by the various state legislatures, the Senate. As James Madison, Thomas Jefferson[4] and many other participants at the convention pointed out the age, citizenship, and residency requirements coupled with the length of office made the Senate seemingly the more stable of the two chambers (Rutland, The Papers of James Madison and Peters, A More Perfect Union).

The framers wanted the Senate to be the premier policy making body because they equated wisdom, deliberation, foresightedness, and moderation as functions of wealth. The House of Representatives was perceived as being populated by persons of lower educational values, less wisdom, and subject to manipulation or bribery. The "vulgar" nature of the House contrasted to the "sophisticated" nature or the Senate, due to the class-based nature of the chambers, was not lost on observers of that era (de Tocqueville, Democracy in America Vol. 1, p. 212). This wish to insure social class representation was

---

[4] Although Jefferson did not participate in the Convention he expressed his sentiments in correspondence with Madison and others.

31

important, as John Dickinson and Gouverneur Morris pointed out, because in the future the less wealthy and uneducated masses would proliferate and probably assert themselves politically. In their perception two chambers would insure that the "aristocracy" would still have significant representation even when the second chamber would come under control of the lower social classes (Beard, An Economic Interpretation, pp. 194-211). The Senate's staidness was supposed to check the democratic tendencies of the House of Representatives. Edmund Randolph best stated this perception during the convention proceedings (Beard, An Economic Interpretation, p. 212). So the only substantive discussions concerning the national assembly were not whether to have one but, rather, how this institution was to be structured in order to insure the hegemony of the moneyed classes. The only other types of state structures, which existed during the late-18th century, were monarchies and the framers had no intention of pursuing that form of government.

The framers saw the need of having some type of executive office that would be responsible for the day-to-day operations of the new government and who could act in an expeditious manner, for instance during times of international crises, when required. This latter factor was particularly important in that it had been one of the principle failings of the Continental Congress under the Articles of Confederation. What the executive would look like became a touchy subject. George Washington found the correspondence of his day openly discussing the possibility of creating a monarchy distasteful and pointed out that the new country would lose face if it chose this option (Beard, p. 58). Some other framers felt that even if a monarchy was not an appropriate avenue the executive should be elected for life as long as he exemplified "good behavior." Charles Pinckney, keeping with his tradition, felt that the President should have a property worth of at least $100,000.

The vast majority of the convention attendees, however, opted for a limited term of office with no limits on the number of terms. Hamilton, in Federalist No. 69, pointed out that what distinguished the presidency from any sort of monarchy was the fact that the " 'magistrate' is to be elected for *four years*; and is to be reeligible as often as the people of the United States shall think him worthy of their confidence" (p. 446). Alexander Hamilton was also quick to point out that unlike monarchs the "President of the United States would be liable to be impeached, tried, and, upon conviction of treason, bribery, or other high crimes or misdemeanors, removed from office; and would afterwards be liable to prosecution and punishment in the ordinary course of law" (p. 446). Hamilton, in Federalist Nos. 69-77, also points out the relationship of the presidency with the national legislature specifically underlining his expressed or explicit powers as being exercised with the "advise and consent" of the Senate. Essentially, these particular essays were designed to point out to the public and to critics of the Constitution the constraints and checks placed on the new executive. This was particularly important in that the young country had just shorn itself of the supervision of a monarch that was perceived as being absolute and arbitrary in many of its actions.

The election of the executive was to be tightly controlled by requiring that the president be chosen by a group of electors selected by each state through a method determined by each state legislature. This process eventually gave birth to what has come to be called the Electoral College and is continuously criticized during every presidential general election year because of the barrier its existence creates between the voting public and the institution of the presidency. Federal law does not require the membership of the Electoral College and each state's political party apparatus tightly controls its composition. Some electors may be bound by their respective state political party laws, to vote for the presidential preferences of the voting public, however, throughout the history of the College there have only been a handful of instances where "faithless electors" have asserted their independence and voted their personal preference over the vociferous objections of the general public (Bickel, Reform and Continuity, pp. 29-34 and Pierce, The People's President, p. 107). Still, the framers constructed this barrier because of their distrust for the judgments of the "common" public and the lower classes of citizens.

It appears from Beard's commentaries and other histories of the federal judiciary that the establishment of this branch was, like the national assembly, a foregone conclusion. Although Beard felt that "the keystone of the whole structure is, in fact, the system provided for judicial control--the most unique contribution to the science of government which has been made by American political genius" (An Economic Interpretation, p. 162). In Federalist No. 78 Alexander Hamilton spoke to the unique role of the judicial branch in the new government pointing out that "In a monarchy it is an excellent barrier to the despotism of the prince; in a republic it (the courts) is no less an excellent barrier to the encroachments and oppressions of the representative body" (p. 503). Hamilton's declaration appears to reflect his distrust of democracy and his perceptions of the lower classes by stating that "in a republic" the judicial branch could be an excellent check on the legislature. On one hand it seems that Hamilton did not intend his statement to mean that the judiciary could act as a check on the presidency, rather, his statement insinuated that the judiciary could, simultaneously, maintain a certain distance from the executive branch. In the same essay Hamilton goes on to speak to the life tenure of the judiciary and their appointment by the president.

There didn't appear to be any debate over whether a judiciary should be considered only its composition and the extent of their operations. Again, some of the framers, exemplified by Charles Pinckney, wanted those eligible to become Supreme Court judges to have a certain amount of material worth. In Pinckney's perception each judge should have an estate valued at $50,000 minimally (Beard, p. 211). Since it was concluded that the appointing process that included nomination by the president and approval by the senate, would obviate the need for the personal wealth parameter it was dropped during the deliberations. Generally, the Constitutional Convention membership assumed that only men of wealth and proper education would appear to the general public as being fit to be members of the executive, senate, and judicial branches anyway so that the question of individual worth was excluded from the Constitution.

The question of judicial review, the Supreme Court's primary function, which does not appear in the Constitution, was bandied about during the Constitutional Convention's deliberations. Farrand pointed out, cited in Scwartz (1993), that there were several options considered and then discarded which would have given the court veto power over legislative actions or have legislation submitted to both the executive and judiciary for consideration before they became law (1937, p. 298). Both options appear to reflect the convention's delegates' fear of democracy again. Nevertheless, as Schwartz points out the foundation for judicial review was embedded in Article III of the Constitution where its declared that "The jurisdiction of the new judiciary extends to all 'Cases...arising under this Constitution, the Laws of the United States, and Treaties." This coupled with the Supremacy Clause which made all laws derived from the Constitution Supreme and the Judiciary Act of 1789 allowed John Marshall to set forth the doctrine of judicial review in the land mark decision Marbury v Madison (1803) which, in turn, would guide all future deliberations of the federal judiciary and provided for another check on both the legislative and executive branches.

The Judiciary Act of 1789 detailed the law that structured the Supreme Court as to its membership, the federal district court system with its collections of attorneys, marshals, and deputies. The Act also set forth the initial appeals processes for carrying cases forward through the judicial system (Beard, The Rise of American Civilization, pp. 339-40). Beard's contention that the judiciary was the most ingenious aspect of the system carries some merit in that the courts have been the most sophisticated structural mechanism that has allowed for the maturation of the American political system. The decisions of the federal courts have played significant roles in extending, protecting, and removing various civil rights which have continuously allowed the political landscape of the United States to weather many social changes. This branch more than any other has fulfilled the perceptions of the modern liberal thinkers when it comes to what they saw as the appropriate function of the state--to moderate conflict among the various competing factions. The courts have both allowed "out groups" to become included into the system; have excluded certain groups to the point that they have no legal standing thus not allowing them to seek redress for perceived wrongs; and, have defined the extent of governmental action and inaction. In short, the federal courts have acted as the "gatekeepers" to political access for many "out groups."

The final distinctive characteristic of the liberal democratic state, which was born in the Constitutional Convention, was the federated nature of the structure. Although one of the "compromises" often spoken of which occurred during the convention proceedings was that between the northern and southern states concerning representation in the national assembly, another aspect of the struggle was propelled by the fear of the states that the national government would gain the power to inappropriately intrude, statutorily, in policy areas where states wished to remain sovereign. There was apprehension on the part of many of the northern and eastern representatives that a delicate balance had to be struck between the powers of the states and the national government in order that one level did not unduly dominate the other. For instance, Madison felt that if the states possessed too much power in one sphere the imbalance could lead to "anarchy" or the "usurpation of national powers." Madison felt the former situation could result if the states possessed too much power while the latter situation could occur if the national government was too powerful (Rutland, pp. 67). The concern over maintaining a balance between the national and state governments which would give the national government supremacy in appropriate areas while reserving to the states those policy areas which were left traditionally to their control dominated the discussions between Roger Sherman, Elbridge Gerry, Charles Pinckney, and John Dickenson on June 6, 1787 (Peters, pp. 60-63). There were fears that if the national government retained too much power the government would eventually tend toward control by aristocracy or, even worse, evolve into a monarchy. On the other side of the argument were those who felt that there was danger that the state governments could be abolished completely. Eventually, language was decided upon that allowed for the supremacy of the federal government in certain areas while insuring the states of a republican form of government allowing them to retain certain powers. The compromise that was struck, however, created a situation where, particularly in the social or political policy realm, it would be difficult to create and implement certain federal laws specifically those perceived as controversial.

A Structural Assessment of the Modern Liberal Democratic State

The framers of the Constitution proved to be ingenious children of their ideological liberal democratic godfathers. The state system which evolved from the Constitutional Convention not only met the specifications required in a modern government by Machiavelli, Hobbes, Locke, Rousseau, Smith, and the Utilitarians in order that a capitalist economy could and would flourish but created a structure that was easily dominated by representatives of the business classes of that historical era. The principle consideration, it appears, was that the government's primary function was to moderate the class (factional) conflict that would inevitably arise from the uneven distribution of wealth in a capitalist society. This would only be accomplished by creating a state system with limited powers to interfere in the daily social operations of the country and by giving the interests of the individual primary consideration over those of any identifiable groups. This balance would allow business to function under loose government controls while, at the same time, maintaining social control over the working and poor classes.

Limiting the government's powers was a deeply liberal democratic belief that Adam Smith and his ideological progeny felt was the only appropriate structural arrangement for the health and proliferation of capitalism. The limitation was accomplished through the fragmentation of the national government by constructing a structure having three branches with each having a distinct realm of authority. These institutional arrangements, nevertheless,

37

overflowed into the authority areas of the other branches creating the possibility of what has come to be known as "gridlock." This overlapping, checking and balancing, tends to dilute or minimize the creation, passage, and implementation of any public policies not favorable to the overall interests of capital or of equalizing the political power imbalance among all groups in society. This institutional fragmentation was exacerbated by the federated nature of the structure where each level of government--state, local, and special--was guaranteed its sovereignty within its specific realm. Additionally, over the lifetime of the United States, each level of government has continued to mimic the diffusion by creating state and local governmental structures that feature the same separation of branches and powers. In short, almost every level of government in every type of jurisdiction possesses a government having executive, legislative, and judicial-type institutions. Te institutional arrangements for these branches are designed like and function similarly to their national counterparts.

Although the separation of branches and the federated nature of the structure are heralded as a strong foundation of democracy in that it makes it relatively impossible for any one faction or individual to gain control of the entire government the feature does have its negative side. The fragmented nature of the government makes it relatively easy for each branch to be dominated separately by those representatives of certain social groups or classes. This is so because the framers constructed a national governmental system in which only one institution, the House of Representatives, was to be open to the representatives of the working or lower classes of property holders, such as small farmers. The United States Senate was to be dominated, until 1913, by individuals appointed or chosen by each state's legislature that was dominated by representatives of each state's upper classes. The executive branch was to be dominated by an individual of stature that could only be achieved through a long life dedicated to business or public service. Dedication to public service has also been used by many individuals as an appropriate avenue for upward social mobility in American society. Still, the presidency was to be filled by an individual chosen by electors who were chosen by the state legislatures of each state and not voted for directly by the people. This insulated the presidency from the people and made the holder of this office subject to the perception that he was beholden to those forces that dominated the local legislative assemblies. Finally, the president appointed the judiciary, already an isolated office holder, and approved by the senate, an institution dominated by the aristocracy. The resulting judicial appointments inevitably reflected the prejudices and perceptions of the dominating classes of American society.

To a certain extent the fragmentation of the government does make it exceedingly difficult for any one group or an individual to gain control of the entire state apparatus, however, because the representatives of the upper classes constructed the structure it gave them a participatory advantage. For instance, Beard points out those individuals who had financed the revolutionary war were present at the Constitutional Convention and insured that specific provisions were inserted in the document so that the new government would repay its rightfully incurred debt. At the same time the framer's fear of the "propertyless" and the "excesses of democracy" allowed them to structure the various branches so that, with the exception of the House of Representatives, the institutions were removed from direct access of the general public.

This structure created a participatory advantage for those individuals representing the interests of those who dominated the national and local economies. By the time the franchise was granted to the general public, the presidency and federal judiciary would be insulated and isolated institutions. Consequently, the interests of capital had a chronological head start of approximately 150 years in which to mold the public policy orientation of the American national government. During this timeframe, the national government had grown dramatically and the United States had grown in international stature economically to the point that it had become a significant "player" in world affairs. The "national" frontiers, which had always been an area where disfranchised groups or individuals could find opportunities that could be parlayed into high standards of living, were closed. The last threat to the integrity of the

39

national character had been turned away during the Civil War and national political power had been consolidated during the Reconstruction era. And, finally, the general social structure of the United States was irrevocably set.

Essentially, the chronological head start for the social classes represented by the framers of the United States Constitution set the political foundation for the social relations which would evolve from the machinations of free market capitalism and the relationship this economy had and would develop with the political structure. The chronological head start would also give a distinctive policy advantage to the interests of those who constructed the government and their progeny and place those who would enter the political system at a later date-- African Americans, women, Latinos, and so forth--in a politically disadvantageous position. This disadvantageous position would guarantee that these groups would be embedded at the lowest levels of American society for a significant period of time because of their inability to access the political and social structures in any substantive and qualitatively meaningful manner. Additionally, these disadvantaged groups would discover that attempting to make this extremely complex and fragmented governmental system respond to their needs would prove almost impossible, if not extremely difficult and frustrating. For examples of the difficulty gaining even a modicum of political access for "out groups" only need look at the histories surrounding the struggles to gain and maintain equal political and civil rights for African and Latino Americans, women, gays, and Native Americans. In some cases protections have been inhibited and/or rejected due to the effects of the difficult and arduous structural processes one must go through to obtain passage of a federal law, win a favorable judicial decision, or amend the national constitution. In other instances, the groups must fight reactionary or conservative elements within their own groups that inhibit the groups ability to appear united on any given issue. For instance where women have their Phyllis Schafley and the "Surrender Woman's Movement," Blacks have their Ward Connoleys, Clarence Thomases, and Colin Powells, and Latinos have their Lynda Chavezes and certain elements of the

40

Cuban Miami communities. Each of these individuals or groups are continuously presented as "counter spokespersons" whenever a civil or political right or legal protection is being sought by members of political out groups to indicate to the general public that these groups are not united in their policy positions or political efforts.

Several other characteristics of the liberal democratic state which allowed it to grow and remain relatively stable over an extended period of time were its ability to socialize conflict and the rather sophisticated socialization process which lent legitimacy to the overall structural and operating processes governing the state structure. The latter was built into the structure through the regularization of elections, setting term limits on elected offices, creating institutional devices which would allow for the removal of "corrupt" or unresponsive officials through means other than the electoral process, the creation and expansion of an institution designed to adjudicate disputes, and the bureaucratic fragmentation of state responsibilities. The socialization process which lent legitimacy to the political structure began with the publicity surrounding the "selling" of the new constitution through the publication of The Federalist Papers and culminated with the transmission of political and social values by the various socialization agents sanctioned by the state, particularly the educational system.

The regularization of elections allowed for creation of the possibility that no one would be elected to office for longer than the period of time deemed necessary to the accomplishment of their charge. Once elected to office politicians could only keep their positions through the dutiful discharge of their duties or acceptable behavior. Once this "public trust" was breached the officials could be subject to removal from office through the impeachment process. One of the most important and profound aspects lending legitimacy to the public trust was the requiring of all public officials to swear a sacred and holy oath to discharge those duties entrusted to them by the people. This clothed the electoral and political processes in the sacred robes of religion and made a violation of the

41

trust tantamount to the commission of a sin against "God." Although this conclusion may appear a bit dramatic it is appropriate when one takes into account the notion that one of the motivating factors propelling the framers to design their new state was to create a system of government based in law. In the liberal democratic tradition this meant that the state apparatus and all those populating the apparatus could not be above the law but were creatures of the law. In this vein Alexander Hamilton, in Federalist 81, pointed out that the function of the judiciary was so structured as to be free to act in the "spirit of the constitution."

The creation of the federal court system, together with the adjudication myth surrounding this institution, is one of the most important devices the American liberal democratic state possessed to socialize any conflict that arose from society. This became glaringly evident during the 2000 General Elections when the courts, both state and federal, became embroiled in the Florida election disputes which culminated in the National Supreme Court being accused by many of having selected Mr. George W. Bush as the winner of the presidency. Additionally, the seemingly endless appeals processes would give one the impression that one's individual rights would be continually overseen and protected by an institution free of political domination and subject only to the "spirit" of the constitution and the laws which would evolve from that same constitution. So that the ethos, the prevailing myth of the federal judicial system, as well as those of all the states, became that the courts were, and are, the foundation of society and the law was nurtured and protected from the meddling hands of politicians and special interests. So the common person was left with the impression that there was always an appeal to be made in their favor to an authority higher than any one person or office.

Finally, the socialization process of the United States became an essential element in the creation of the legitimation of the state. This process became responsible for the transmission of liberal democratic values, including the acceptance of social inequalities and justifications set forth for the international involvement of the military. Socialization began and is still maintained through the control of the school curriculum, the expression and propagation of patriotism through religious institutions and the media, and the control of and management of a class-based ideological social structure. The latter is evident in the creation of public policy positions in areas as diverse as urban economic development activities and the decisions of the federal judiciary. Many of the political actors who create and implement ideologically based public policies or legal decisions affecting the substance of the public policy debates are not aware of the ideological biases of their perceptions and actions because they have been lifelong subjects of the socialization processes of liberal democratic society as have their parents, teachers, and mentors before them. Nonetheless, this socialization process began in the churches, schools, and media of the colonial era, has proliferated and become more and more sophisticated at the same rate that the liberal democratic state and society have developed.

In the final analysis the contemporary liberal democratic state which exists in the United States of America was given its form, its structure, by the composers of the Constitution who developed the political structure from the principles of liberal democratic thought which evolved from the thinking of Machiavelli through Adam Smith and his contemporaries and followers. The state system was not designed to do anything concerning the creation of a democratic society where all persons are equal in every sense of the word but was designed to protect the economic system championed by Adam Smith. In the perception of the framers, a "myth" still perpetuated and expounded, the market mechanisms of capitalism would eventually spread wealth to all sectors of society. All liberal democratic thinkers, including the framers of the Constitution, were well aware that social and political inequalities were a logical consequence of capitalism and that the inequalities were capable of causing social tensions and possibly violence. Consequently, the liberal democratic state's structure had to be one which guaranteed protection for the interests of the dominant social and political classes while, at the same time, providing for the mystification and the protection of the inequalities that the economic system would give birth to.

Chapter Two

The Structural Barriers
Of the
Liberal Democratic State

The initial state structure that the framers of the Constitution created evolved over the next two hundred years into a complex matrix of institutions and institutional arrangements that have come to manage efficiently the social inequalities created by the machinations of capitalism. Management of the political inequality that exists within a liberal democratic society is left in the hands of the state, the private economic sector, and the relationship between the state and the economic sectors. All three sets of institutional arrangements create structural barriers to the social and political betterment of those classes and social groups that came late to the political structure or were included in the political structure through force. In this latter category one finds African and Asian Americans, Latinos, and all other groups whose homelands were subjugated by the United States, or because of the United States' intervention in their part of the world, and were forced to enter this country either legally or illegally.

The inequality spawned by the private sector is the direct result of several factors. Fundamentally, social and political inequality is caused by the exclusion of a particular groups' interests during the decisional processes of institutions at all levels of society. One of the principal reasons this exclusion occurs is because the excluded classes or social groups do not have access to significant amounts of capital or the types of resources required to take advantage of the types of investment activities from which one can derive large profits. This situation results in the excluded groups being continuously relegated to the lower rungs of America's social structures because they cannot take advantage of those investment decisions. These groups will, for the most part (there always be some individual exceptions) find themselves among the poor, working poor, or working classes. Reinforcing this strict social hierarchy is the fact that the vast majority of African Americans and Latinos are also excluded from the highest circles of the corporate and social world where all of the investment and organizational decisions are reached that dictate the direction of the American economy.

The second set of institutional arrangements insuring the maintenance of the social inequality inherent in the United States is the unique relationship enjoyed between the public and private sectors. The nexus between the state and the marketplace within a liberal democracy is extremely complex in that it is multidimensional and is interwoven throughout the state's public policy formation and implementation arenas. The precise nature of the public policy structure is determined by ideologically defined principles based upon a three hundred-year-old perception of how a liberal democracy's society should be structured. The public/private nexus, however, is not benign in that it structures or organizes the relationship between the state and the marketplace in favor of the interests of those controlling the marketplace. The complexity of the relationship makes managing those groups and classes at the lower rungs of the social structure very easy, in fact, it has become almost a self managing process. Nevertheless, the relationship between the private and public sectors are complex and difficult to untangle because the lines between both sectors have become blurred over time; the true nature of the relationship has been mystified through the propagation of the "cult of pluralism;" group conflict which, under pluralism, no longer exists; and, group interaction assumed always to be equal (Lustig, 1982).

Lustig points out that although the lines between the public and private sectors were clear at the beginning of the republic they have become blurred to the point that one finds it very difficult to discover exactly where one can draw the

45

line between the two in contemporary liberal democratic society. The blurring is such that it has made conceptualizing about the state very difficult. His second point, that the true nature of pluralism, as a way of defining the manner, in which power is shared in liberal democracies, has been misconstrued. This appears to be the result of overuse of the term and the inability to move beyond a superficial level of analysis by many champions of the term. Nevertheless, the general understanding of pluralism is that power can be shared easily and it sees authority constituted from below. The reality, however, of the political world is that the United State's political landscape is dominated by elites and authority is a reflection of pluralistic interaction by groups of elites which dominate each group that they represent.

Additionally, group conflict, an essential ingredient in pluralism's recipe, no longer exists. What has replaced group conflict is orchestrated interaction among groups dominated and organized by society's elites. Social stability although perceived as the result of group interactions, cross-pressured loyalties, and overlapping memberships is, in reality, "a product of executive leadership and administrative engineering." The leadership is executed as a result of the partnership between private and public sectors in almost all policy arenas with the policies being the result of negotiation and bureaucratic and organizational algorithms. The leadership will determine what are the important foci of or for society while the algorithms give birth to the policies and programs, together with their parameters, required to implement these programs.

Lustig's last point, undergirding the relationship between the public and private sectors, is that although group interaction is always assumed as being equal it is really highly unequal. Some organizations and groups have access to larger amounts of resources than others making power relationships asymmetrical. This situation arises because society allows some groups to become larger and more powerful than others. Either the group's functions are defined in such a manner that growth is inevitable and/or this function is assisted by the state by granting "humanhood" to corporations and allowing for the proliferation of "unchecked mergers."

The nexus between the marketplace and the state, between the private and public sectors, is best expressed ideologically by the continuous espousal, on the part of politicians, citizens, and bureaucrats alike, of a partnership between the public and private spheres creating a "corporatist form of rule" (Lustig, 1982). As Lustig points out the marriage between the state and the marketplace is not historically unique to late capitalist societies rather state apparatuses have always been manipulated to protect some one's or some group's economic hegemony. What is unique to liberal democracies is that the current relationship between the public and private sectors is one that classical liberal thinkers could not and did not envision.

According to Lustig, the two spheres have become fused during the last two centuries because the private sector has gained control of public sector responsibilities (Reagan, 1963) and have infiltrated the public policy formation process at all levels (Lowi, 1969; Dye, 1990, and, Domhoff, 1969). The fact that the private sector maintains almost absolute discretion over locational, production, and distributional decisions and their consequent impact on the standard of living of the general population, affects a government's ability to provide certain public and/or municipal services. The principle reason for this is that the discretion exercised by private sector decision makers substantively affects a government's ability to generate tax revenues in order to provide the type and quality of services the public expects and demands (Lindblom, 1977; Flores, 1989).

Private groups also possess "the power to circumscribe constitutional rights, to assign duties and impose sanctions for the breach of them, and to create obligations enforceable in the courts" (Lustig, 1982). In this latter arena one of the most significant occurrences during liberal democracy's evolution was a gaining of "human status" by corporations. In the United States a corporation is a person under the law possessing almost all of the privileges and fundamentally protected liberties of the individual person. Essentially, a corporation is legally

47

equal to a person before all courts in the United States that guarantees corporations the same freedom of expression and right to petition the government as each individual citizen. This also allows a corporation to receive benefits from the state when necessary to avoid economic death, to exercise freedom of speech in order to mold public opinion, and to sue anyone in a court of law for any apparent slander (Miller, 1976). Corporations recently began pursuing the strategy of countersuing those groups or individuals who have brought suit to correct industrial pollution. The legal entanglements become so expensive that citizen or consumer groups think twice before pursuing such law suits (New York Times, 1989).

Finally, the third set of institutional arrangements that create barriers to the political empowerment of those groups, and here the discussion will be limited to Latinos generally and specifically Mexican Americans, are the structures of the state itself. One way in which this particular problem can be perceived is by applying the framework formulated by Claus Offe (1975). Offe suggests that "selective institutional mechanisms" operate within any state apparatus to filter out policy alternatives that are considered politically unacceptable. Specifically, the filtering process may exclude events in three ways: (1) by structuring social attitudes and value systems so that an event may never arise, for instance in a capitalist society one will never hear of the nationalization of the oil or banking industries as viable policy alternatives to alleviate crises confronting those sectors; (2) by creating economic development scenarios in which governments always plan for growth in "partnership with the private sector," never considering the possibility that in some situations planning for no growth may be more compatible with the local economy and environment; and, (3) by systematically excluding events not perceived to be endemic to society but rather reflective of the weakness of human beings, such as poverty, racism, sexism, hunger, and unemployment. The difference between the first and second situations is that the former is principally caused and manipulated by the normal socialization processes so that possible policy alternatives are generally unconsciously or subconsciously excluded from the policy dialogue. This type of exclusion results because decision makers are not taught or trained to conceive of policy alternatives that violate society's norms. Generally, these types of policy alternatives are not compatible with the values taught to decision makers in schools of business or public policy and are very rarely topics of discussion among professional groups except by academics or thinkers who are quickly labeled radicals or, at least, "non-practical" thinkers. The second situation is different in that the policy alternatives arising under this scenario do arise during policy discussions but are "logicized away" as being too costly, inefficient, overly complex, or in some way unimplementable.

Offe's selective institutional mechanisms become institutionalized at every governmental level. The policy choices which are left, after all of the decisional algorithms and machinations are completed, are declared to serve the economic/social structure as a whole, rather than the parochial interests of any one individual or group, thus giving the entire process a democratic façade. Conceptually, selection mechanisms appear throughout the political superstructure, however, they are concentrated at three specific levels of the public policy process: bureaucratic and political structures and decisional processes; ideological formation and maintenance systems; and, public policy implementation processes. Essentially, the public policy process is structured along specific ideological lines that are based on liberal democratic principles such as limiting government, the primacy of the individual, the fragmented nature of government, and so forth. These principles determine the scope and degree of governmental action throughout the policy process from the creation to the implementation stages. The manner in which institutions at every governmental level are structured and operate acts as a filtering process creating barriers to the empowerment of Chicanos.[1] Although at first glance one might argue that, given the effects of the first two institutional arrangements, politically empowering

---

[1]Throughout this volume I will use Chicano interchangeably with Mexican American and Latino, however, as the data will indicate I am principally speaking of persons of Mexican descent residing in the United States.

49

Mexican Americans has limited efficacy. Latino electoral participation and success is very important, however, because one way of pursuing partial solutions to the social inequality of liberal democracies is for excluded groups to gain a seat at the public policy table. This means gaining access to and a certain degree of control over the political apparatuses in order to clear up the blurred nexus between the private and public sectors and making the private sector more responsive to the needs of society generally.

Bureaucratic and Political Structures

The bureaucratic and political structures of a liberal democracy are barriers to the empowerment of Latinos because they place finite limits on which matters and issues can and will be dealt with by the governmental apparatuses and political processes. For example, constitutional and legislative guarantees defining civil liberties result in statutory protection of private property, freedom of speech, the right to vote, and the right to hold office. Although these concepts stand as pillars of any liberal democracy, the manner in which they are perceived, interpreted, and implemented can actually create institutional barriers to Latino empowerment.

For instance the right to own property by an individual is perceived as a desirable liberal democratic value and encouraged at all levels of society. Nonetheless, the exploitation of private property during the economic development processes normally pursued in large urban centers mitigate against the individual property owner and in favor of those who can collectively pursue land development investments. This collective exploitation is possible, partially, through the extension of "person status" to corporations by the federal judiciary. These judicial decisions extend Fourteenth Amendment protections to corporations creating institutional barriers that generate a competitive advantage for corporations over the average person. The private corporation's social standing within the business community again gives it an additional position of privilege because it enhances the corporation's ability to tap the requisite amounts of capital necessary to manipulate large investment efforts.

The bureaucratic and political structures possess two facets, which may be labeled ideological and substantive. The ideological facet of the barrier, which will be discussed later, refers to the manner in which every political actor interprets a given concept that eventually leads to the definition of policy parameters. For example, the manner in which the ownership of land is conceptualized by various sectors of American society determines who will be successful in almost any significant economic development scenario. The virtues of the collective ownership or control of large tracts of land, where the scope and location of development determines the degree and certainty of capital gains and profits, are not revealed to subgroups such as migrant farm workers, the under employed, unemployed persons, and single heads of households. Albeit, this information also is denied to individuals of any social class not affiliated with the appropriate corporate circles, however, this essay focuses only on Latinos and persons of less than middle class social status. Instead social subgroups which understand both virtues of and how to exploit the collective ownership of land such as domestic and international corporations, land developers, and venture capitalists take advantage of the collective ownership of land to accumulate vast amounts of wealth.

Obviously, Chicanos are overly represented in those subgroups whose only understanding of land ownership and exploitation is based on individual as opposed to collective ownership. In other words, concepts such as collectivism are understood and utilized by the private sector to control the economic development process while the same concept is not made available to working and poor communities. Instead, the poor are taught that individual initiative and ownership are the appropriate values for successful participation within a capitalist economy. Nowhere in their socialization are the working and poor classes taught the virtues of cooperative or collective economic initiative. It is not that Latinos are consciously denied information concerning the viability of collective ownership or control, rather, it is simply that the ideological formation selection mechanism weaves competitive-individualism so deeply into the socio-

51

philosophical tapestry of society that Chicanos, searching for strategies to overcome economic institutional barriers, will seldom consider creating collectives large enough to compete in the marketplace.

The substantive facet of the bureaucratic structures of the state apparatus, specifically at the local governmental level where economic development policies are created and implemented, perceives and defines developmental activities as the traditional avenue leading to the solution of many local social problems. The selection mechanisms determine how economic development problems and issues are defined and which geographical areas are given developmental priority. The prioritization process eventually leads to uneven developmental patterns reflected by sharply defined residential segregation patterns in almost every city in the United States. Uneven development and egregiously divided living patterns are particularly evident in San Antonio, Texas: a city having by far one of the largest Mexican American communities in the Southwest.

The first characteristic of the barrier is the manner in which the economic development problem is defined. For example, it is assumed by both public and private sector officials that "stimulating economic growth" can solve all economic problems, such as unemployment, inflation, poverty, and so forth   In turn, economic growth is measured in several ways: economic output, number of jobs created, increases in median incomes, increases in sales, and so forth. Within a capitalist society, however, responsibility for economic production, measured as growth, lies not in the hands of the public sector but in those of the private sector. The locus of responsibility in this decisional structure acts as a barrier against the interests of Latinos in San Antonio because the investment decisions driving economic development will qualitatively favor the interests of those making the decisions as opposed to those whom cannot even participate in the process. In effect this leaves the resulting economic status of Latinos in the hands of corporate decision-makers. The end result is that unless the corporate decision makers place the interests of Latinos at the forefront of their developmental planning, then the interests of the Latino community will be excluded completely, included as an afterthought, or relegated the lowest priority.

Decisional Processes

Like the decisional structure, the decisional processes of liberal democracy also act as selective barriers to the Chicano community. Some of the processes include (1) the formal rule structures determining the algorithms of legislative consultation, (2) collective-bargaining and mediation/arbitration arrangements, (3) bureaucratic planning and administration, (4) policy discussion by academic experts, (5) election campaigns, and (6) political mass communication which predetermines the possible content and outcome of the process. Superficially, the process mechanism appears as an objective, formal, orderly manner of reaching public policy decisions. In reality, however, the rules invest certain policies with increased chances of being "implemented by providing certain interests with a head start, and by granting them [the interests] chronological priority, relatively more favorable coalition chances, or the opportunity to employ specific power resources" (Offe, 1975, p. 40). Complicating the decisional process is that it can operate consciously and deliberately or it can be used to implement the non-decision making process described by Bachrach and Baratz (1962).

On a more specific level, the economic developmental decisional processes, which are institutionalized within the bureaucratic and political structures of liberal democracies, act as barriers to Chicano empowerment as they exacerbate the already poor economic conditions of the Mexican American community. The point is best illustrated through a brief description of the bureaucratic decisional processes governing the direction of economic development in San Antonio, Texas. A more detailed and extensive discussion of economic development politics in San Antonio will be presented in Chapter Four. Nevertheless, this brief example is crucial here as it underscores the question of whether electing blacks or Chicanos to "major" political offices *really serves as adequate* minority empowerment.

53

In San Antonio, economic development policies create programs that exclude the participation of groups other than those possessing, controlling, or having access to large amounts of investment capital. Furthermore, not being in the social position to "play" the private sector's investment game also excludes Chicanos from participation in the public bureaucratic decisional process. This is true because, operationally, the decision making process is so complex that the average Mexican American citizen, if aware of the process at all, will become confused and withdraw from participation. Additionally, even if either the public or private sectors solicit participation in alternative economic development options, such as the possibility of joining collectives or cooperatives as alternatives to individual participation, the state or market representatives will not identify the options as viable. Essentially, the alternative developmental programs will be deemed inefficient, unprofitable or not serving the needs of the entire community. In the final analysis, any economic development, that occurs in what are considered low-income areas of San Antonio, is geographically smaller than in other areas, requires smaller amounts of investment monies, and results in relatively lower returns on the investment. Over the long run, these smaller investments also result in relatively lower property values because the value either remains the same or deflated in relation to those of higher values in other areas of the city. The decisional structural bias insures that the low-income areas of cities remain relatively underdeveloped compared to the more affluent areas. Here an overview of how San Antonio prioritizes the use of land for economic development will suffice to substantiate my contention. In a later chapter this discussion will be expanded in greater detail.

Economic Development Prioritization in San Antonio (Bureaucratic Structure and Process)

Developmental decisions in San Antonio appear to be based upon private sector investment assumptions, are subject to the manipulation of developers and financiers, and result in unequal developmental outcomes. San Antonio has no formal planning process per se, instead developmental decisions are reached through negotiations between developers, investors, the city's planning commission, and the city council. It appears that the only variable affecting whether a particular parcel of land will be subjected to developmental activity is whether the activity will violate any specific zoning ordinance or federal or state environmental law. Essentially, San Antonio has operated over the last forty years without a formal developmental plan. What this has resulted in is unfettered developmental activity occurring in those areas of the city that private developers deem suitable. Growth patterns mirror investment decisions and only occur in those geographical areas possessing higher land values and in areas where the residents enjoy higher incomes. These growth patterns, characterized by rapid population expansion and the proliferation of commercial districts to the northwest and northeast quadrants of the city and away from the central business district (Jones, R.C., 1983, 48; Flores, 1989) are substantiated by the fact that between 1990 and 1995, 83% of new home production has occurred in the Northeast and Northwest Quadrants of the city (San Antonio City Planning Department, 1995).

The effect of San Antonio's developmental decisions is to increase the value of land in the north while land values in the city's other quadrants remain the same or have a tendency to decrease. The data reflecting the differences in land values in the northern and southern quadrants of the city are displayed in Table 2-1. As the data indicate the property land values for single family housing in the northern tier of the city have consistently risen over the fifteen years covered in the table, while those in the southern tier have remained significantly lower. Additionally, housing values in the south have been erratic, at best, increasing some years while decreasing in others. If one considers the value of housing as an indicator of growth, then, the significance of these growth patterns is twofold. Representatives of business interests who controlled the local developmental process made the decisions that directed the growth and their decisions affected only the northern tier of the city. On the other hand, the areas of the city not experiencing growth, excluded from developmental consideration,

55

are those neighborhoods possessing significant proportions of the city's Chicano population. Given this brief example, it appears that the economic development structure and the assumptions dictating developmental decisions are biased toward the interests of the business sector in both cities. Meanwhile the developmental policies of San Antonio appear to perpetuate the undervalued or underdeveloped condition of those areas at the lower end of the developmental priority list. Since these underdeveloped geographical areas house the vast majority of Latinos, one must conclude that the social and economic status of this group is not likely to improve in the near future. This social and economic situation may be a primary factor for the structuring of Chicanos into the lowest rungs of America's social structure and could contribute to relegating Chicanos into a type of permanent underclass.

Table 2-1

Single Family Residential
Development in Bexar County
1980-1994
Property Tax Accounts (Parcels)

Year	Northern Tier	Southern Tier
1980	121,150 (47.2%)	135,580 (52.8%)
1985	147,250 (49.8%)	148,289 (50.2%)
1990	157,580 (55.8%)	124,682 (44.2%)
1994	176,674 (56.4%)	136,706 (43.6%)
2000	222,315 (58.7%)	156,169 (41.3%)

Average Value
Single Family Residential Accounts

56

1980	$73,206.72	$30,656.16
1985	$80,402.68	$30,620.13
1990	$83,334.82	$35,803.67
1994	$88,375.77	$31,850.22
2000	$99,215.87	$44,269.12

Source: San Antonio, TX. Bexar Appraisal District. "Schools: State 'Self' Reports." 1982, 1985, 1990, 1994.

Incorporation of Minority Mayors (Political Structures and Processes)

The biased nature of the developmental structure notwithstanding it has been assumed that if racial minority group members are incorporated into the city's political structure they would be able to mitigate, to a certain extent, the economic problems of the low-income minority communities (Marshall, Browning, and Tabb, 1984). However, in order to win election to and stay in office, Henry Cisneros, the Chicano mayor of San Antonio, who first won the mayoralty in 1981 and held office for eight years, had to gain access to and support from, the local business community. Inevitably this meant that Mr. Cisneros, regardless of how he felt concerning any issue, had to support the economic development priorities of the private sector.

Not only did Cisneros represent a city experiencing unprecedented economic development and growth over the last forty years, he had to run and win campaigns in a political culture rife with racism. For instance, although approximately 60% + of San Antonio's population is Latino, it is generally conceded that almost every Mexican American politician will have to develop his or her electoral tactics to account for the extreme racial polarization displayed at the polls. In other words, there is significant statistical evidence, which will be presented in great detail in a later chapter, that Anglos (Whites or Caucasian) voters do not vote for Mexican American candidates in high proportions.

57

Conversely, Chicanos do not vote for Anglo candidates but prefer to cast their ballots for Mexican American candidates. This "rule of thumb," known in voting rights litigation research as "racially polarized voting," has held consistently true throughout the Southwest since data of this sort has been collected (Davidson and Grofman, 1994; Davidson, 1990). Nevertheless, it is a general assumption that to compensate for the extensive racial polarization, at least in San Antonio elections[2], a Chicano candidate must either have the blessings of the business community who will champion their cause in the media and to other factions of the private sector or face the consequences of only receiving no more than a small percentage of the Anglo vote. In this latter situation the Latino candidate is faced with the task of enticing the Mexican American community to vote in larger numbers than are normally achieved because, although representing the majority population in San Antonio, Mexican Americans vote at lower rates than Anglo voters. Henry Cisneros has been the only Chicano politician who has been able to "cross over" and gain the requisite business support while enjoying great personal favor among the Chicano and general community. The most important ingredient, however, for Mr. Cisneros was gaining the valuable business support.

Mayor Cisneros' initial election to the San Antonio City Council was gained as a member of a slate of candidates endorsed and supported by the Good Government League (G.G.L.), a reform machine, in 1975. The G.G.L. was formed in late 1954 to insure "stability and integrity in city government" and was founded by local businessmen, attorneys, and "other professionals and clergymen" who resided in the "silk-stocking neighborhoods of the north side" (Booth and Johnson, 1983, p. 23). The G.G.L. would support a slate of candidates who were prosperous, lacked further political ambition, demonstrated "civic mindedness," and represented the "community as a whole," eschewing strong partisan or ethnic allegiances and working for growth and economic expansion (Sanders, 1975, pp. 14-17).

---

[2] The author has testified in over 40 federal voting rights lawsuits and has found that similar racial polarization patterns exist throughout the state of Texas at many jurisdictional levels. Racial

In 1974, however, several events caused an upheaval that transformed the face of San Antonio politics for at least the next decade. A difference of opinion concerning long-term economic development philosophy caused a rift among G.G.L. notables. Some wished for very slow growth concentrated within the confines of Interstate Highway 410, while others wanted unlimited expansion northward of the same highway. Interstate 410 is known locally as "The Loop" for it encircles San Antonio proper and until the decade of the 1980s conceptually separated the city of San Antonio from the County of Bexar. After 1980 development became so intense that the city of San Antonio had grown well beyond "The Loop" and threatened to take in the entire county and small portions of several adjoining counties. Currently, many refer to the inner city as that area inside "The Loop."

Those who favored the slower, more conservative growth scenario represented the older business establishment while those championing the latter perspective represented the newer, younger land speculators and developers. Additionally, the agitations of a coalition featuring environmentalists and a Saul Alinsky-type inner city, mostly Latino organization, Citizens Organized for Public Services (C.O.P.S.), politicized many municipal service and economic development issues (Sanders, 1975, pp. 95-113). Finally, the implementation of the Voting Rights Act of 1965 resulted in the elimination of the at-large election structure and the birth of a single-member district election process (Sanders, 1975, p. 102). This latter situation was of primary significance in that, for the first time in the history of San Antonio politics, members of the Chicano community dominated the city council. This in itself would make San Antonio and its politics unique among large American cities.

Henry Cisneros's arrival on the San Antonio political scene at that precise historical moment, was a fortuitous occurrence for many organizations and political actors feuding over various local issues. From the late 1960s until 1975, San Antonio's political environment was a cauldron of strife. There were

polarization is particularly pronounced in rural areas but is still significantly evident in the large cities such as Houston and San Antonio.

accusations of city council members receiving questionable campaign contributions. There was the fact that "the city had been paying the Greater San Antonio Chamber of Commerce roughly $1 million a year to attract new industry" (Diehl and Jarboe, 1985, p. 55). There was a scandal within the City Public Service Board that sent monthly utility bills skyrocketing. And, there was the fact that city government had consistently overlooked the inequitable distribution of municipal services. Into this South Texas political "prairie fire" walked Henry Cisneros

> who has walked the line between the requirement of responding to and speaking for the Hispanic community of San Antonio and the need to enlist and retain the support of the city's business leaders. Too little zeal on behalf of the former would damn him as the Chicano version of an "Uncle Tom," too much militancy would lead the latter to question his "soundness" (Diehl and Jarboe, 1985, pp. viii-ix).

After running for and winning a city council seat as a member of the last official G.G.L. slate in 1975, Cisneros declared his independence by overtly supporting positions unique to the Chicano community which allowed him to position himself for the mayoralty. His effort was dictated by several strategies that included gaining the support of both the business and Chicano communities. The "glue" which held his unusual coalition together was his perception of economic development. Mr. Cisneros believed that the most significant approach to uplifting the relatively depressed socioeconomic conditions of the Chicano community was to create a "healthy" economic environment, within the confines of that community. On the other hand, Cisneros understood that the key to maintaining a healthy economy was to create conditions that allowed the local economy to expand and economic expansion relied solely on the investment decisions of the business community. Mr. Cisneros' perception has been characterized as "double fisted" in that his approach to the paradox was to create a partnership between government and business working together to create jobs for the unemployed [which] sometimes gets him crosswise with both conservatives and liberals. Conservatives sometimes criticize him for supporting government programs. Liberals sometimes mistrust him for being a cheerleader for the free enterprise system (Diehl and Jarboe, 1985, p. 8).

Although Cisneros' philosophy was neither realized nor understood until several mayoral terms, according to many observers it is evident that his position remained consistent throughout his tenure as both a city council member and Mayor of San Antonio.

The 1981 mayoral election, Cisneros' first, was a landmark in San Antonio power politics in that for the first time since 1842 a Chicano was elected to office and the behind-the-scenes power shifted from the older, central city oriented business community to the younger developers, bankers, and entrepreneurs who wished to see the city economically expand beyond any foreseeable limits. One young developer perceived the election in the following manner: "What this election is really about is the Oak Hills Country Club versus the San Antonio Country Club and us Oak Hills boys are going to beat the hell out of the old guys" (Diehl and Jarboe, 1985, p. 74).

This same developer became the link between Cisneros and the "new guys" convincing the remainder of the "Oak Hills boys" that this young Hispanic shared their perception of economic development and would also serve as a communications conduit to the Latino community (Diehl and Jarboe, 1985, pp. 71-74). A perusal of Mayor Cisneros' contributions lists reveals that between 1981 and 1989, the business community, particularly those "Oak Hills boys," gave liberally to his support. Admittedly, it is difficult to draw conclusions about those who contribute, the amounts of contributions, and specific public policy decisions made in favor of those contributors. However, this correlation would only be important if Mayor Cisneros supported generally non-business oriented public policy decisions. Instead two things must be kept in mind. First, San Antonio literally exploded economically during Mayor Cisneros' tenure. Almost every significant economic indicator has shown improvement and/or increases. For instance, the number of jobs available in the local market continued to increase even during the severe national recession of 1981-82; San Antonio's unemployment rate showed a steady decrease during the same time frame; per capita income grew more rapidly than the nation's; and, the amount of available office space doubled between 1982 and 1984. A study by Ricecenter (1985), a Houston-based community research and development corporation, concluded that "San Antonio's Economic Development Program (created with Mayor Cisneros' initiative) is considered to be the general issue that is being most adequately addressed currently."

This brief example of the appropriate placement of economic development decisions within the general public policy decisional arenas of San Antonio together with the relationship of that locus with what minority mayors must "do" in order to win election leads one to several conclusions.

-The economic development decisions are almost solely in the hands of the private sector.

-Local governmental planners must plan the use of land for economic development generally coincident with the private sector's investment decisions because of where the decisional locus lies.

-Racial polarization and anti-liberal bias causes minority mayors to champion the private sector's economic development philosophy in order to gain the requisite support in order to win election.

-The minority mayor's economic positions coincide generally with those of the business community because the decisional locus lies almost entirely in the hands of the private sector.

All of the above conclusions can be summarized by simply stating that the structure of the private and public sectors are inextricably intertwined to such an extent that any minority mayor who decides to champion non-business positions

62

in large American cities will most likely be doomed electoraly. Additionally, Lindblom's perception that the private sector's economic development decisions drive the government's and not vice-versa looms as largely at the local governmental as it does at the national or international levels (1977).

The Public Policy Implementation Process (Structurally Imposed Decisional Parameters)

The public policy implementation process creates an additional barrier to Latino empowerment. This selection mechanism's inherent bias is controlled by choice limitations embodied in the constitutions, statutes, codes, and ordinances guiding government activities in almost every policy arena affecting the social and economic well-being of the Chicano community. Probably the most insidious barriers to Mexican American empowerment are constructed by those jurisdictions having interpretive responsibility, because interpretation determines the implementation method. These latter organizations include all levels of the judiciary and any bureaucratic agency possessing broad discretionary powers.

Chicano labor history offers many examples of state bureaucratic agencies using police and military forces to suppress dissent (Acuña, 1981) and thus denying Chicanos influence in certain private sector decision-making circles. In these cases, Chicano workers were denied access to collective bargaining arrangements by both private industry and the traditional American and International labor unions. So that Mexican American workers always were subject to the policy arrangements either dictated to them by industry or by the Anglo union leaders who held racist perceptions of Chicanos generally.

Nevertheless, the overt repression historically aimed at the Mexican American laborer is overshadowed by the repression resulting from certain legal rulings imposed by the Federal judiciary. This is particularly evident in the decisions rendered by the Supreme Court of the United States in the areas of education and voting rights. These two policy areas are particularly important to Chicanos because they have been the traditional avenues that Mexican Americans have perceived for generations as appropriate byways through which to participate and become part of American political society.

In San Antonio Independent School District v. Rodriguez 411 US 1 (1972, 29), the high court ruled that wealth discrimination does not provide an adequate basis for invoking strict scrutiny the highest level of judicial activism normally reserved for such cases as discrimination in education and voting. This ruling essentially made it impossible for poor persons generally to seek the protection of the court because the court did not recognize an easily identifiable class of poor persons. It's not that the court denied that certain persons subsist below the federally defined "poverty level" it simply refused to recognize that a "class" of poor people existed in the United States. This is tantamount to relegating the poor to legal invisibility! If they have no legal standing then they cannot bring a lawsuit as an identifiable group or class; if they can bring no suit then they are denied access to one of the major political institutions of the American state.

The lack of standing notwithstanding, Rodriguez was a class action suit brought by a Chicano parent, "on behalf of school children throughout that State who are members of minority groups or who are poor and reside in school districts having a low property base" (Rodriguez, 1972, p. 5). The suit was brought against the Texas State Attorney General and the Bexar County Board of Trustees. The suit claimed that the Texas school financing system was unconstitutional under the Equal Protection Clause of the Fourteenth Amendment because school districts possessing lower property values found themselves unable to generate revenues equal, even taxing at higher rates, to those of wealthier school districts. Specifically, the Edgewood Independent School District, located on the near westside of San Antonio and having a student body approximately 90 percent Mexican American, at the time of the suit, possessed the lowest assessed property value per pupil ($5,960) and the lowest median family income ($4,686) in the metropolitan area. Unlike the Edgewood district, the

64

Alamo Heights Independent School District, the most affluent school district in the county, had property assessed in excess of $49,000 per pupil and a median family income of $8,001 (Rodriguez, 1972, pp. 12-13). The suit contended that the difference in assessed property values per pupil, coupled with the state's tax structure, discriminated against school districts possessing property of lower value. The fact that reliance on property taxes as the primary basis for generating school revenues created unequal funding opportunities for poor schools was the crux of the lawsuit.

The court's decision was based on several points, none of which focused on the inequity of the private property system that was, and still is, the central aspect of the entire issue. The Court concluded that "wealth discrimination" did not provide "an adequate basis for invoking strict scrutiny" except where one class could pay absolutely nothing for a constitutionally protected service, which was not the case with respect to education (Rodriguez, 1972, p. 29). The Court admitted that the Texas school financing scheme was "unfairly structured" although "only relative differences in spending levels are involved." The Supreme Court concluded that the education system does not "fail to provide each child with an opportunity to acquire the basic minimal skills necessary for the enjoyment of the rights of speech and of full participation in the political process" (Rodriguez, 1972, p. 37).

The Rodriguez decision was not only a devastating blow to the possibility that the public educational system would begin treating Chicanos equitably and fairly but the decision's language carried far greater consequences. The court denied that any "definable class" of poor persons existed generally and that education, although required by state mandate, was not a constitutional right. So the decision not only rendered Chicanos, as members of an economic class, legally invisible it also shut the constitutional door on the one institution that Mexican Americans have traditionally viewed as essential to achieving "the good life" in the United States--education. By declaring that education was not a fundamental right to which access is protected by the constitution, the Supreme

Court stated, in no uncertain terms, that one couldn't seek judicial relief in this policy area for any perceived civil wrongs. The Court logicized their position by stating that the children were not absolutely denied access to education but were receiving the minimal attention necessary as defined by the state to be able to participate in the American political process.

If the court had moved beyond legal thinking/reasoning it would have become apparent that the court was not completely accurate in their conclusions concerning the relationship between socialization and political participation. The basic conclusion that a positive relationship exists between education and political participation is, in itself, accurate (Wolfinger and Rosenstone, 1980). Where the justices went awry was that they failed to understand that the quality of education, reflected in the students' intentions to pursue higher education, depends upon the families' affluence, educational levels, and 'the cultural benefits of their higher status" (Haveman and West, 1953). Langton and Jennings concluded that

> indeed, students who plan to attend college are more likely to be knowledgeable about politics; to express greater political interest and efficacy; to support religious dissenters' rights of free speech and an elected communist's right to take office; to read about politics in newspapers, in magazines; to discuss politics with their peers; and they are three times as likely to place the correct liberal-conservative label on the Democratic and Republican parties as are those students who are not planning to pursue a college education (1968, p. 867).

Consequently, sitting in a classroom exposed to the "minimal skills necessary for the enjoyment of the rights of speech and full participation in the political process" is not enough to make for a well-informed electorate. Having a quality education which stresses social advancement, exposes students to various avenues for achieving social success in society, and enlightens students on the intricacies

66

of a political structure as complex as liberal democracy and results in quality political participation. Less quality in education will most likely result in an electorate who will not participate or vote, or at least minimally, and who will be politically ill informed and susceptible to unscrupulous propagator (Giroux, 1988). James Madison pointed this out in Federalist 10 and Thomas Jefferson also feared the politics of an uninformed electorate. Whether access to the appropriate socialization research would have changed the court's mind is only a matter of speculation. Regardless, the court's ruling relegated education to the realm of privilege and allowed the maintenance of a publicly financed socialization system that can only result in Chicanos remaining among the ranks of the economically, socially, and politically disadvantaged.

In the educational policy arena, then, the Supreme Court's decision created parameters around what was and is available to Latinos when it comes to pursuing increased quality. Since education is not a fundamentally protected right, Mexican Americans, at least, cannot expect federal protection in seeking any improvement in this policy arena. Any redress, therefore, must be pursued at the state and school district levels. Which in the case of Edgewood and other poor school districts is exactly where they began. In 1987 a class action lawsuit was filed against the State of Texas, in the state court system, by every "poor" school district in the state including Edgewood. After all the appeals, the State Supreme Court found that the state financing scheme violated the Texas State Constitution's clause which stated that the state must provide for "an efficient system of free public schools" (Edgewood ISD, et al v Kirby, et al, C-8353, 6). During the intervening years various financing schemes have been devised to answer the court's demands that the financing structure be rearranged in order to meet the constitutional mandate. To date there has been some improvements in the quality of education Chicano children are receiving on the westside of San Antonio. Nevertheless, one still finds dropout rates among primary and secondary school students exceeding 50%, poor quality teaching and over crowded classrooms. Jonathan Kozol dramatically described these dismal conditions in San Antonio westside schools in his award wining Savage Inequalities.

Ideological Formation and Maintenance Systems (Sociologically Imposed Decisional Structures)

The most sophisticated selective mechanism and consequently the most difficult to define, to discuss, and to change, is the structure and mechanics of the ideological formation and maintenance systems. The problem lies in the sophistication and abstractness of the ideological system. Once institutionalized the system goes unarticulated, permeates the institutional structures, and governs the selective perception and articulation of social and economic problems within the political process. This ideological selective mechanism biases both the perception of those controlling social, economic, and political institutions and also the perception of the institutions' clientele. The selective perception causes those in power to define social and economic problems and their solutions from an extremely narrow perspective, and causes the people, subject to the dictates of those in power, to accept the rationalization for their social and economic conditions. Additionally, selective perception allows for society to generally accept the rationale for any possible solutions to their problems that come forth as policy alternatives from the system. Sometimes dissent is expressed, however, generally this occurs within legitimate social settings, following socially sanctioned rules of communication (Offe, 1975). Maintenance and formation of ideology acts as a particularly insidious barrier to empowerment because it occurs throughout the socialization process. As a result the imposition of an ideological belief structure on a population goes almost totally undetected and unchallenged throughout one's lifetime by either the subject (the receiver of the socialization) or the transmitter.

The institutionalization of a specific ideological framework within the structures of various state apparatuses results from the fact that humans bring to bear a certain perception of the social, economic, and political world when dealing with a specific issue. This perception includes everyday attitudes and

68

experiences, elaborate intellectual doctrines, and "the consciousness" of other social actors, and the institutionalized thought systems and discourses of a given society (Therborn, 1980, p. 2). Thus, "the operation of ideology in human life basically involves the constitution and patterning of how human beings live as conscious reflecting initiators of acts in a structured, meaningful world" (Therborn, 1980, p. 15). Ideological interpolation, which most humans experience when confronting a given social situation, includes identifying a phenomenon and concluding what should or should not be done in relation to that phenomenon (Therborn, 1980, p. 2). In the political arena this translates into voters making choices among politicians and/or issues, politicians choosing how to stand on a given issue, and bureaucrats defining problems, creating solutions, and implementing public policy based upon narrowly defined ideological values. In the end, only public policies designed to identify socioeconomic problems from an extremely narrow and biased perspective are considered for possible action. If it is predetermined that the problem merits attention, then only solutions acceptable under the restrictions of the dominant ideology are considered for possible implementation.

Ideology, if viewed as an interactive process rather than an object that is transferred from one individual to another, causes individuals to not only develop a conceptual and perceptual framework through which they can interpret the political and every day world but ideology also prepares one to act within those worlds. So that political participation then becomes the end product of ideological conception, perception, interpretation, and interpolation. In turn, depending upon one's place within the social structure, an individual can transmit their ideological perception to others through various sorts of communications media such as during the teaching/learning process. In the public policy arena, specifically in the case illustrated above, the bureaucrats, politicians, financiers, developers, justices, and others who participated in either the economic development decisions of San Antonio and in arguing and deciding the Rodriguez case argued their positions along ideological lines.

69

In the realm of economic development the bureaucrats and politicians viewed the economic world, as did the investors, as a place to pursue profits within a free market environment. The government joined together with the private sector to develop a broad plan and then the private sector completed the work of investing, building, and selling. In order to obtain participation of the developers and financiers the bureaucrats were required to plan using similar assumptions that investors use. If these assumptions were not met then the city government risked losing potential investors to other cities. The politicians, in order to get elected as in the case of Henry Cisneros, even having a commitment to change the direction of a city's economic health, can do no more than to go along with the private sector's economic development perception or else they will fail to gain the much needed electoral support of the local business community.

In the Rodriguez case the judges reached their decision on strictly ideological grounds such that throughout the text there is an unconscious acceptance of the existence of poor persons within capitalist society while at the same time a refusal to admit that definable poor classes exist within liberal democracy. This, in itself, reveals an interesting liberal democratic contradiction in that there is a refusal to accept that extreme economic and social differences exist between social classes within society while at the same time accepting the notion that individual social conditions will be unequal within the same society. Placing the emphasis on the individual as opposed to a group or social class. This reflects the socialized preference (belief) for the notion that individual initiative will solve the economic plight of Latinos as opposed to considering a policy position that would assist an entire group or class. This ideological preference is the evolutionary offspring of one of the belief "principles" of liberal democratic thought--individualism." Individualism, although praised at all levels of a liberal democratic society, mitigates against collective action and may be a threat to the advancement of diverse groups from the family unit to the racial group to the social class (Stewart, 1988, pp. 88-93). Simply placing individuals at odds with

70

one another, while immersed in the soup of a competitive culture creates a tension that mitigates or subverts any attempt at either collective thought and/or action.

Additionally, like the framers of the constitution, the Supreme Court in Rodriguez threw the "people" a crumb, admitting that there was something wrong, allowing them to appeal a complaint to the highest authority, and then saying that although they were an injured party they really were not totally incapacitated so they were still able to participate in political society. This is tantamount to a judge ruling against an injured party, in a personal injury law suit, stating that although the injured party had lost a hand, due to the negligence of the defendant, they were not completely incapacitated because they still possessed one hand. This sort of paradoxical, if not out rightly hypocritical, behavior has historical precedent in that similarly, in an earlier historical era, the framers pretended to give the people access to one of the highest institutions of the government by making election to the House of Representatives appear to be open to all eligible voters with minimal qualifications. In both cases, full participation was denied yet possible conflict was averted because the masses were allowed to vent their complete frustrations through one of the political access channels. In the first instance the people were allowed to petition the courts; in the second the people were allowed to cast a vote for some candidate. Both types of political access lead the petitioners and voters to believe that they have a substantive role to play in the political process and, consequently, enjoy a certain level of acceptance by the political institutions and the players controlling those institutions and processes. In both instances, however, the petitioners and voters channel their political frustrations through the acceptable, legitimized political access channels, the courts and voting booths, rather than taking up arms seeking revolutionary or violent change or redress. Nonetheless, the court's decision in the Rodriguez decision simply resulted in Chicanos having to achieve educational gains under the same poor conditions that they began in.

Then, the earlier discussions concerning economic development and judicial interpretation illustrate, to a certain extent, the manner in which ideological interpretation and bias can and does affect the selective perception of individuals. In both cases there was no evidence that the politicians, bureaucrats, or justices considered policy alternatives that were diametrically opposed to those predominating in American society. The insidious nature of the ideological selection mechanism causes those making decisions automatically, seemingly unconsciously, to exclude policy alternatives deemed to be politically, socially, and economically unpalatable. This insures that the system of values and norms dominating the United States determines what is the proper subject for state action, which necessarily preconditions how teachers teach, how police and judges interpret the law, and how urban planners plan the use of land for economic development.

Structure, Ideology, and Public Policy

The liberal democratic state is both an artificial and conceptual construct. The state is an artificial construct because it is the creation of humans who intentionally set down a structural foundation to govern a society for very specific reasons. The framers of the Constitution set the precedence that governed the construction of all other governments within the United States when they structured the national government in the manner that they did. Although the ethos of local government control existed prior to the Constitutional Convention and many state and local governmental structures existed prior to the reconstitution of the national government in 1787, most governmental construction, however, has occurred during the two hundred years since the writing of the Constitution. Since then, the liberal democratic state has become more fragmented[3] and, consequently, power has become more diffused throughout the entire federal structure. Nevertheless, the liberal democratic state was constructed in such a fragmented manner in order to specifically control the potential conflicts that may arise within liberal democratic society. Essentially, the fragmented nature of the federal system allows for the creation of an almost

---

[3] Fragmented is understood to be a combination of decentralization and the separation of responsibilities among many branches of government where the authority and sovereignty appear

72

unlimited amount of political access channels through which political frustrations and challenges can be funneled. It appears that the more fragmented, yet very well organized and controlled, the political system, the more political conflict can be diffused.

Adam Smith felt that the structure had to be specific to the type of society that would be spawned eventually by capitalism and his perception indirectly manifested itself at the Constitutional Convention. This perception is what makes the state a conceptual construct because it represented a conception, an idea, if you will, of how government should be constructed in order to properly govern within a liberal democratic society (Foucault, 1991). Essentially, conceptualization of the liberal democratic state as to "what" constitutes the state, "what form" the state takes, and "what defines the state's parameters" will give birth, when implemented, to specific state constructs. This is true because each state construct depends upon the actions of particular political actors responding to or reacting to an infinite number of factors under, most often, unpredictable circumstances (Foucault, 1991, p. 4). If one assumes that both the conceptualization of and the state's structure are deliberately oriented in a particular manner for a specific intention then it can be concluded that both are ideologically defined because conception depends upon one's life experiences and one's socialization. The framers of the Constitution were the ideological godchildren of liberal democratic thought and constructed the government of the United States upon principles derived from their ideological perception. These same principles of fragmented and limited government were transmitted to later generations of American political actors through the traditional socialization mechanisms and found their way into the processes that gave birth to every state and local governmental apparatus and institutional arrangement.

The institutional arrangements of late capitalist society, particularly the one between the public and private sector is a descendant of the classical liberal democratic thought of Adam Smith, Thomas Hobbes, John Locke, Jean Jacques

---

to overlap and jurisdictional boundaries are sometimes overlapping, sometimes confusing, sometimes clearly demarcated.

Rousseau, the Utilitarians, James Madison and Alexander Hamilton. Although the private/public nexus is designed to achieve some economic development end, whether at the national, state or local political levels, it also is designed to achieve two other goals. The first goal is to insure a chronological and decisional head start to private sector interests and, secondly, it is intended to insure both a modicum of legitimation for governmental policies. The latter goal is also supposed to insure the social control required for the smooth operation of the state apparatus.

The two very brief cases presented above give one a hint of the biased nature of the liberal democratic state's structure. The structure itself is ideologically determined because its jurisdictional scope is limited by the dominant value systems. The public generally assumes that the government is the leader in any policy arena. In some policy areas it does, particularly when it comes to dealing with crisis situations such as during time of war or while attempting to combat crime. The remainder of the time, however, the state follows the lead of the dominant value systems of its society. In the economic development policy arena regardless of whether one is referring to the national (Lindblom, 1977) or the local (Flores, 1989; Judd, 1988; Stone, 1989; or Elkin, 1987) political levels the state always follows the dictates of the private sector. It is not that the private sector overtly demands certain concessions from the state, although this does happen at times, its simply that most often the public and private economic planners are basing their plans on the same assumptions. This is not serendipitous thinking rather the effects of schooling and exposure to the same professional standards that dominate their day-to-day operations (Vasu, 1979). Essentially, similar, almost identical interpretations of the economic world cause both the private and public planners to develop their investment and land use plans along similar lines.

One can conclude, then, that the political and bureaucratic structures that form the state apparatuses are ideologically determined and manipulated to generate policy outcomes that serve the general interests of society. These general

74

interests, in turn, are determined by the dominant ideological orientation of that society. When looking at liberal democracies and how they determine public policy decisions that directly affect the social well being of Mexican Americans one can reach several conclusions. First, the interests of Chicanos as a whole, defined in this discussion as achieving higher levels of social advancement, are not the same as those of the dominant society. If it were the case that the interests of the Latino community were coincident with those dominating the decisional structures of the state then the development plans would have emphasized those programs compatible with the interests of the Mexican American community. Additionally, the economic development policies would be designed where the Chicano community could become, at least have the opportunity to become, important players in the business and corporate communities. Finally, the judges in the Rodriguez decision would also have ruled quite differently if they had the interests of the Chicano community foremost in their minds. The court would have declared that public education was a constitutionally protected right and demanded that the state of Texas take positive steps to equalize educational policy so as to begin laying the foundation for improving the social and economic lot of Chicano children. Instead the judges apparently relied upon the rather fallacious American notion, myth if you will, that a prosperous private economy will, in the long run, solve any social or economic problems that may exist throughout society. As a result where one discovers poverty it is either the fault of the individual suffering poverty level conditions or a temporary condition that will disappear as this individual works "hard" and reaps the fruits of American social wealth. The judges refused to consider the possibility that American society is a class based society with little movement between class levels (Domhoff, 1990; Dye, 1984; Wright, 1985).

The biased nature of the state structure notwithstanding the next question that must be asked is why and how the state evolved in the manner it did during the last two hundred years and why is this evolutionary process important to understand. The key to the evolution of the state from one form to another may

75

also provide the key to understanding how Latinos may achieve a certain degree of political power at the local political level. The complexity of the national state coupled with the numbers of Latinos, and their diverse cultural composition, prohibit discussing whether they can ever achieve national political power. A national presence is possible together with the ability to influence national policy to a certain degree, however, gaining national power is not possible in the foreseeable future.

Chapter Three

Chaos Theory
and the
Evolution of the State

The question that almost all state theorists have failed to address or, at least, failed to address completely is "what is it about the state that causes it to evolve from one form, or variation, to another over time?" What has been overlooked in the discourse thus far is the notion that the state is not a "static construct" but its form (structure[s]), governing processes, and definition are constantly changing. The inability even to consider the state as a "dynamical" system[1] has prevented the spokespersons of the various "state schools" from achieving closure on this topic. My position is that *the state is in constant flux, taking on different forms during different historical eras, resulting in differing policy outcomes.* Additionally, it is my perception that existing theories of the state are incapable of providing a rationale for this fluid conception. This perception is not unique in that it is derived from certain principles borrowed from what has come to be known popularly as "Chaos Theory."

Chaos Theory: A Brief Introduction

Chaos Theory, generally the purview of physicists and mathematicians, was born in an attempt to understand variations in some physical systems that appear random "even though their behavior is in fact determined by precise laws"

---

[1] "Dynamical," the adjectival form of dynamic is borrowed here from the chaos theory jargon for its connotative "flavor." It gives one an impression of fluidity, constant changing, that the term "dynamic" simply doesn't.

(Lorenz, 1993, p. 4). Originally, chaos theory was not a theory but a declaration on the part of certain investigators who kept observing disorderly behavior in mathematical and weather systems that should not have occurred given the constructed algorithms. Why this phenomenon came to be known as chaos and how it became a "theory" are not matters for discussion here. What is important to the discussions concerning the theory of the state is that certain principles that have become synonymous with chaos theory also appear to be applicable to the state theory dialogue. Whether the entire theory can be applied and tested as an appropriate "substitute" for other theories of the state is not clear as yet. Certain principles of chaos theory, however, may allow one to answer, at least partially, the questions concerning the nature or form and the limits of the state.

The fundamental principle underlying chaos theory is that nothing in the universe, particularly human-made constructs can be completely understood because of some innate imperfections that are overlooked or misunderstood by investigators or designers. In the social sciences Lindblom (1990) has discussed this notion and the cause of this situation in great detail. The resulting consequences are that one is able, with only a certain degree of accuracy, to predict or control the short-term behavior of any occurrence. Even more disconcerting, particularly to economists, is that undetectable systemic imperfections result in the inability to understand or predict long-term behavioral patterns.

Prigogine (1984) identified this problem best when he set forth his theory of change. Ilya Prigogine, a physicist who won the 1977 Nobel Prize for his work on the thermodynamics of non-equilibrium systems, contends that one can understand and predict some parts of the universe because they are closed and one can control and identify every variable affecting that system. The vast majority of systems comprising the universe, however, are not closed but are open "exchanging energy or matter with their environment" and any "attempt to understand them in mechanistic terms is doomed to failure." He suggests that this is particularly true for biological and social systems.

78

Prigogine's notion rests on the foundation that all systems are composed of subsystems continually fluctuating because of the effects of variables both internal and external to these systems. Lorenz feels that only those systems affected by changes caused by internal variables should be included in the chaos family because, he was speaking of physical systems, all systems are limitless or they possess infinitely defined parameters (pp. 22-24). Lorenz's position, when applied to social systems, would have to be modified greatly in that the parameters of the state can be considered as both finite and infinite. This is a crucial notion and requires clarification particularly when attempting to define the parameters, the limits, of the state within a political system like the United States where the interaction between the local, regional, state, and national states is extremely complex. To identify an external variable in such a complex society where every governmental level and jurisdiction affects every level of society becomes almost impossible. Nonetheless, the fact that sometimes externalities produced from the action(s) of one state to or on another requires that one includes the effects of external variables on a state as an essential element of the formulation considered in this discussion.

In Prigogine's perception at various times some predictable and others not, the fluctuations of one variable or combinations of fluctuations cause the system to arrive at, what he has labeled, a "bifurcation point," or a "singular moment." At this precise moment "the system will disintegrate into 'chaos' or leap to a new, more differentiated, higher level of 'order' or organization...." This new level or order is called a 'dissipative structure" simply because the new organization is much more sophisticated than the previous structure while at the same time possessing elements of the previous structures.

Katherine Hayles, a literary critic and professor of literature at the University of Iowa who also possesses a background in chemistry, in Chaos Bound: Orderly Disorder in Contemporary Literature and Science (1990), besides presenting an excellent overview of the theory including contrasting "schools"

79

within Chaos Theory,[2] adds the notion that chaos does not have to be seen as a void, an absence of order, but rather as a "positive force." That culture can be seen as an "archipelago of chaos" where various areas of culture are inextricably bound together, intersecting at various points. She utilizes this metaphor to describe the intersection of chaos theory, post structuralism, and contemporary fiction.

It is appropriate to use a similar metaphor to discuss the intersection of a broad array of factors or forces which comprise a political matrix, within which lie systems, structures, and processes, arranged in such a way as to give the matrix a definitional essentiality to which a population can relate. Some matrices, depending upon the manner in which the systems, structures, and processes are arranged, have been defined as totalitarian, authoritarian, democratic, and so forth. By assuming that these political matrices are dynamical or nonlinear entities, however, one can better understand why the systems, structures, and processes change form; why, and how, the systems, structures, and processes rearrange their relationships to each other; and why, and how, individuals and/or groups of individuals, subject to these matrices, interact with these matrices. Included in this latter area are various methods and manners of political orientation to, and participation within, the relevant political matrix.

Hayles points out that there appears to be two schools of thought within Chaos Theory. The first, represented by Prigogine, indicates that the focus of chaos theory is "on the spontaneous emergence of self-organization from chaos; or, in the parlance of the field, on the dissipative structures that arise in systems far from equilibrium, where entropy production is high." The assumption of this school is that entropy, rather than leading to disorganization, facilitates self-organization. So that order can arise from chaotic systems; rather than chaos

---

[2] Hayles points out that Chaos Theory includes the work of researchers in such diverse fields as nonlinear dynamics, irreversible thermodynamics, meteorology, and epidemiology where researchers prefer using the term "nonlinear dynamics" rather than insinuating that anything is chaotic. To this school the use of "Chaos Theory" or "The Science of Chaos" "signals that one is a dilettante rather than an expert." (1990, p. 8).

leading to more chaos, chaos gives birth to order. This notion is the linkage to post modernity as interpreted by Lyotard.

Essentially, Lyotard contends that modern structures, from linguistic to social, possess, within their structures, the seed or catalyst for change. There is something inherent and specific to the modern structure that will cause the structure to change either dramatically or ever so slightly in order to accommodate the forces of the changing world around it. Lyotard calls this situation or modernist characteristic "the postmodern condition" and the moment of change "the postmodern moment." The old order will give way to a new order that, in turn, will experience the same situation at some undetermined future moment (1984). So the postmodern moment is simply a period during which change occurs not, necessarily, an historical era succeeding the modern era or even an "anti-modernist" moment (Turner, 1990).

In discussing the evolution of the contemporary city, David Harvey, in his ground-breaking work The Condition of Post-Modernity (1989), posits that the postmodern condition is caused by the social and economic contradictions specific to capitalist development. Harvey suggests that the very characteristics unique to capitalism, "the coercive laws of competition and the conditions of class struggle endemic to capitalism" (p. 105), underlie the dynamic nature of this type of economic and social system. So that expansion and growth place strains on their subsystems, such as ecological, financial or social, that consequently places pressures on the entire social structure. Both the state and society must somehow change structurally to accommodate these pressures. These structural accommodations, in turn, cause either or both the state and social system to change their form and/or their institutional relationships. It goes without saying that the physical form of the city will also change as a result of the same developmental forces.

The other chaos theory school of thought "emphasizes the hidden order that exists *within* chaotic systems. Chaos in this usage is distinct from true randomness, because it can be shown to contain deeply encoded structures called

81

'strange attractors'." Strange attractors are points in space, for physicists phase space or the space within which a phenomenon is occurring, that are not fixed yet are essential definers of the system. Where attractors are periodic, occurring as essential points or elements of a system, for instance climate is an attractor of weather, strange attractors are those points that are non periodic occurrences of a system. Kauffman adds a refinement by indicating that some strange attractors are stranger than others. In other words some systems may experience different dimensionalities of chaos than others (1993). Regardless of the degree of chaos, strange attractors change the definition and the form of the system. Essentially, the first Chaos Theory school of thought perceives order emerging from chaos, while the second school sees chaos caused by the order in a system.

It appears that the conclusions of both schools of thought may be applicable to state theory. On one level chaos can give birth to order for example in those cases where an existing state is overthrown through revolutionary means and another state replaces the displaced state. In the second case an overly ordered state, if it never changes, may eventually be reduced to a chaotic condition. The inflexibility of the state in the latter example results in the inability of the aging institutions and processes of the state to socialize or identify conflict which may result in an extreme reconfiguration of the state's form or in the state's demise.

Characteristics of Chaos Theory

Although Hayles points out that there are few "connections" between the two schools of Chaos Theory, there are certain characteristics or principles common to both from which political science can learn much in attempting to develop a more thorough understanding of the state. Before identifying these principles, however, it is appropriate to set forth a working definition of Chaos Theory. Prigogine, shunning the term chaos, sees the theory as a "comprehensive theory of change" which holds "that while some parts of the universe may operate like machines, these are closed systems, and closed systems, at best, form only a small part of the physical universe. Most phenomenon of interest to us are, in fact, *open* systems, exchanging energy or matter (and, one might add, information) with their environment. Surely biological and social systems are open, which means that the attempt to understand them in mechanistic terms is doomed to failure" (Toffler, 1984, p. xv). Continuing, Prigogine concludes "that most of reality, instead of being orderly, stable, and equilibrial, is seething and bubbling with change, disorder, and process"(Toffler, 1984, p. xv).

For Prigogine this means that all systems contain continuously fluctuating subsystems and that, on some occasions, a "single fluctuation or a combination of them may become so powerful...that it shatters the preexisting organization." At this "singular moment" or, as Prigogine states, this "bifurcation point," it is impossible to "determine in advance which direction change will take: Whether the system will disintegrate into 'chaos' or leap to a new, more differentiated, higher level of 'order' or organization" (Toffler, 1984, p. xv). Prigogine appears to insist that order or organization can spontaneously arise out of disorder through a process of self-organization within the system.

Scientists from many fields appear to agree that "complexity flourishes" in the physical world. That regardless of the physical system in which one is performing research one will encounter unexplained oscillations or fluctuations that cannot be explained by traditional laws of physics or mathematics. Research has uncovered the observation that, unless one has an extremely controlled environment, all systems are dynamical, changes over time, and are dramatically affected by forces at various times in their lives. James Gleick feels that the convergence of the research findings from fields as diverse as astronomy, neurology, ecology, meteorology, epidemiology, entomology, and metallurgy, among others has led to the possibility of the creation of a "new science," the science of chaos (1987).

What all the researchers do not have in common is what to call the new field. Below is a sampling of some of the labels that have been used by physicists or mathematicians to describe what the study of chaos is.

-The complicated, aperiodic, attracting orbits of certain (usually low-dimensional) dynamical systems. Philip Homes, Mathematician.

- A kind of order without periodicity. Hao Bai-Lin, Physicist.

- Apparently random recurrent behavior in a simple deterministic (clockwork-like) system. H. Bruce Stewart, Mathematician.

- The irregular, unpredictable behavior of deterministic, nonlinear dynamical systems. Roderick V. Jensen, Physicist.

- Dynamics freed at last from the shackles of order and predictability.... Systems *liberated to randomly explore their every dynamical possibility....* Joseph Ford, Physicist. (Gleick, 1987).

Gleick points out that all who have attempted to describe the phenomenon and give it a name have generally agreed that chaos is too narrow because it implies randomness when, in fact, sometimes complexity could arise without randomness.

The working definition of Chaos Theory for purposes of this essay is that "dynamical systems experience aperiodic structural changes, in varying degrees, due to the unintended effects of variables internal and external to the systems." This definition varies dramatically from that discussed by "hard scientists" in that it includes the "unintended effects of variables internal and external to the systems." This definition is designed in a manner that it can be applied to the study of the state in that it assumes, that in the world of politics, government, and states, an essential characteristic of the state is that all states possess certain degrees of sovereignty or autonomy. The sovereign nature of the state coupled with the place of the state within an international or national context, depending on whether one is speaking of the local state or a state of a higher order, places this type of system in a unique category in that it takes on characters of both open and closed systems. For instance, in the United States local states--city councils, county governments, special districts, and so forth--have complete sovereignty and legal control over certain functions. Simultaneously, authority over certain other state functions is shared with other governmental entities. An example of a local state's sovereignty is a city government's "legal" or "statutorily based" right

84

to manage the day-to-day operations of its police force. At the same time the police force is constrained, theoretically, by state and federal civil laws concerning "due process" and "equal protection" measures. In this case the parameters, boundaries between the local governmental actors and the constraints of the state and federal statutes, is often determined by the discretionary judgment of the police and/or the judicial system. So then the issue of whether the state is an open or closed system is not as clear as in the physical sciences. As a result, in a definition of chaos theory applicable to state systems one must include the notion that the system is subject to the effects of both internal and external variables.

Principles of Chaos Theory

The definition of chaos theory chosen for this essay "dynamical systems experience aperiodic structural changes, in varying degrees, due to the unintended effects of variables internal and external to those systems" possesses certain principles or characteristics that must be discussed before presenting an application of the theory.

States are Dynamical Systems - The definition assumes that the state is dynamical. In other words the state is not a static construct but changes from one historical era to another. The rearranging of structures or institutional arrangements comprising the state manifests this change. Some structures will disappear altogether if they are found to be obsolete, others will grow larger, others may metamorphose into completely different structures, and still others will be created to meet new needs or state emphases.

Structural Changes are Aperiodic - The structural changes that the state undergoes occur at indeterminate moments in time and may occur during a transitional period which may last a number of years. One may not be able to accurately predict the length of this transitional period and/or when this period will occur. This transition period is equivalent to what physical scientists call "bifurcation points" or the moment in time where a number of forces converge causing a chaotic reaction or the rise of a strange attractor. When speaking of the state the strange attractor is the appearance of a structural arrangement which is both born

85

from the system, because of the effects of some variable(s), but also a structural arrangement that was not quite what political actors expected to arise given the "normal" or "traditional" patterns of past political occurrences. This latter phenomenon will be made clear when the application of chaos theory is presented later in this chapter. The important thing to keep in mind here is that any changes that occur to the state are aperiodic so that they are unpredictable and occur at irregular intervals.

Structural Changes are Unintended - Generally speaking the structural changes that occur due to the activities of various political actors within or outside of the state cannot be accurately identified or predicted. This is a function of human nature, on one hand, while at the same time it is also a function of the system's structural nature. Lindblom, most recently, has pointed out that humans only have a limited capacity for identifying and manipulating all data possibly required in order to identify and solve social problems. At the same time all dynamical systems, particularly the state, are so complex and their structures are so determined by past historical occurrences, that it becomes impossible to appropriately identify the sources of a specific social problem let alone the problem's solution. However, if one is able to come close to identifying the problem and its solution then the politics governing the internal and external dynamics of the system together with any appropriate systemic structures will significantly change the substance of the proffered solution. This is readily seen in the manner in which the national legislature functions. It is subject to an array of variables, bureaucratic, parliamentary, partisan, and self-interests so that any one item of legislation is either buried never to see the light of day or is so changed that it is but a mere shadow of its original self. The same complex matrix of barriers control and limit any possibilities of substantive change in the electoral, judicial, and bureaucratic institutions and processes of the state.

The System is Subject to the Forces of Both Internal and External Variables - The internal variables of the dynamical system include the political actors themselves together with whatever actions or activities, rational or irrational, may result from their everyday normal behavior or behavior caused as a result of a crisis situation. Additional examples of internal variables include every aspect of the socialization processes that manipulate the political and social attitudes, opinions, and perceptions of all political actors. Internal variables must also include all laws, ordinances, statutes, constitutions, regulations, customs, traditions, or other types of guidelines that determine the manner in which institutions are structured, how they function, and how the general population is expected to interact with the state. So then, internal variables are any factors that may affect interactions within the state resulting in any state action.

External variables are those that find their origins outside of a specific state's jurisdictional or conceptual boundaries and directly or indirectly affect the state's behavior. These variables may be the result of actions taken by another state, whether part of the same larger dynamical system, as in a federal arrangement, or from an entirely different system, such as the actions of another nation state or group of states. An example of the latter category may be the effect on the United States' foreign policy posture given internal decisions by Japan's national government or the actions of the European Community.

So then, a state must be considered a dynamical system in that its structures and processes, and even its populations and constituency groups change from one historical period to another given the effects of variables both from within and outside of the system. These changes occur at irregular intervals but they do and will occur. The depth and intensity of the changes depends upon the depth and intensity of the effects the system is undergoing and the ability of that system to incorporate, absorb, or repel the effects. If the system is unsuccessful then it will experience dramatic change, it may even disappear and another will take its place but appear dramatically different structurally; if the system is successful in absorbing the effects of the variables then it will change structurally ever so slightly, however, in the long run these minute changes will eventually result in a system which appears dramatically different than when it was originally created.

Chaos Theory and the State

To date the various discussions and debates concerning what constitutes the state and what causes the state to change form have turned on conceptual disagreements. These discussions are not limited to the national state but include the urban regime as well (Stone, 1989). These disagreements have centered on how one defines the locus of power within the state apparatus and gave birth to the now famous instrumentalist versus structuralist debates of the 1970s and 1980s. One side of the debate was led by Ralph Miliband who envisioned the state as an almost benign entity subject to the dictates of those who gained political control of the apparatus (1969). This rationale eventually gave ideological birth to the Eurocommunism movement of the 1970s where it was felt that gaining electoral control of state apparatuses would allow communists, and their allies, to create public policy that would be able to eradicate poverty and political inequality, protect the environment, and control imperialistic capitalist expansion that was devastating lesser developed countries. Nicos Poulantzas who argued that the foundation of a society determined the orientation of a society's "superstructure" (1968) led the structuralists. For Poulantzas, gaining political control was only one step if, in fact, winning electoral control of the state was an appropriate step given the nature of a capitalist society's societal structure. The only thing, however, that would lead to qualitative changes in the public policy process was a restructuring of the state, down to its very foundation. The debate between the two schools of thought openly raged for almost fifteen years with each argument and counter argument advancing knowledge of the state one step further. Yet, in the end neither side was declared the winner and the various parties appeared to simply lay the argument aside for another day.

The only notable non-Marxist thinker who attempted to substantively intrude in the fray was David Easton (1990), but he succumbed to the same conceptual error that, it appears, the Marxists did. No one attempted to understand the state as a dynamic, complex system subject to various changes at any given moment within any historical period for any number of explained or unintended reasons. Only Greenberg (1990) seems to have attempted to understand that the form a state assumes is subject to any number of changes both from within and without. Nevertheless, there appears to have been a failure to seek to place the theory of the state within a broader theoretical framework. It is my perception that chaos theory has given us this opportunity.

The theoretical assumption of this chapter's discussion, then, is that *the state is a dynamical system and, consequently, experiences aperiodic structural changes, in varying degrees, due to the unintended effects of variables internal and external to the system.* I intend exploring this proposition using the evolution of the San Antonio, Texas political environment as the evidentiary base. Nonetheless, I suspect that this analysis can be extended to every type of state system within any given society. Because the state is a dynamical system its form is subject to a broad array of constantly changing variables including changing social values, attitudes, political practices and beliefs, institutional schemes, economic structures, social conditions, and the behavior of various elites to name a few. In turn, each of these variables are affected by many and sundry other variables affecting the manner, together with the degree of intensity, in which these variables affect some aspect of the state. This phenomenon, known in the jargon of chaos theory as the "Butterfly Effect," generally results in a second or third order effect which was unintended by whomever initiated the original action. In public policy literature this has been labeled as a "spillover effect," "economic externality," or an "unintended consequence."

"The Butterfly Effect," simply stated, is the notion that dynamical systems are heavily dependent upon the initial conditions of the systems. Lorenz found that the smallest perturbation in initial weather conditions could lead to very large conditions after many iterations. The origin of the name of the effect, according to Lorenz, is unclear other than the word "Butterfly" appeared in the paper where he posed the theoretical question in 1972 (1993). In the paper entitled "Does the

Flap of a Butterfly's Wings in Brazil Set Off a Tornado in Texas?" Lorenz posed the following propositions.

> 1. If a single flap of a butterfly's wings can be instrumental in generating a tornado, so also can all the previous and subsequent flaps of its wings, as can the flaps of the wings of millions of other butterflies, not to mention the activities of innumerable more powerful   creatures, including our own species.
>
> 2. If the flap of a butterfly's wings can be instrumental in generating a tornado, it can equally well be instrumental in preventing a tornado. (1972).

Although Lorenz was speaking metaphorically, the implications are clear. The actions of any variable or collection of variables at anytime can dramatically affect any system. These forces will produce any number of changes within the system causing it to behave in a completely unintended manner. On the other hand, the fact that something did not occur also has an unintended effect on the manner in which a system is structured and how, subsequently, it operates.

On a general level Lorenz's metaphor applies as equally to the social and political worlds as it does to the weather patterns he was attempting to understand. For instance, Lorenz feels that weather patterns, although showing some periodicity, are generally unpredictable. One can predict some weather patterns, it may rain, snow, and so forth tomorrow, for example, however, exactly where and precisely how much precipitation will result is impossible to say. The weather may even reverse itself and decide not to rain or snow even if every indicator has led prognosticators to predict so. This apparent erratic behavior is caused by the effects of multitude of variables exerting different types and degrees of intensities of pressures on the initial conditions. Additionally other, sometimes unidentifiable, effects will change the weather patterns as it progresses throughout the atmosphere. This continual and unpredictable "bombardment" causing the unpredictable weather patterns is what Lorenz labeled the "Butterfly Effect."

90

Like weather patterns and other physical systems and structures, social systems and structures are also subject to sometimes erratic and unpredictable forces that eventually result in dramatic changes to the initial effect or during the processes of construction or maturation. The major difference in the systemic or structural changes caused by the effects of the forces on social systems is that they are caused generally by the actions of human beings. Additionally, the changes may not be as immediately apparent as in weather systems because, sometimes, minute or incremental forces such as a single budgetary decision that may take a decade to reach fruition cause the changes. Some changes to social systems may occur over centuries such as the rise and demise of the Roman Empire. Other social systems may change practically instantaneously such as when Czarist Russia passed from the scene in 1917 to be replaced by a dramatically different social system. In both cases change was caused by the actions of political actors and resulted in the restructuring of the political, economic, and social systems in Rome and Russia.

Lorenz's metaphor is applicable to this discussion in that what we find as the leading causes of racial segregation in San Antonio, Texas is the result of the evolution and subsequent implementation of what Adam Smith propagated in his Wealth of Nations. To Smith's credit he saw that unbridled capitalism would lead to social inequalities. Essentially, he felt that individual greed could lead to extreme uneven accumulation, which, in turn, could lead to massive social unrest and, in the end, provide the basis for a threat to capitalism. In Smith's perception the inequalities would be caused by the dual effects of the division of labor and manipulation of investment activities in England and Western Europe. Regardless of Smith's foresight he did not foresee that these same two effects would affect development activities in San Antonio, Texas. Nor did Smith foresee that the inequalities he feared would translate into racial segregation residential patterns that, in turn, would translate into an eventual call for equal political representation on the local city council. This call would result in a federal voting rights law-suit that resulted in the imposition of single member electoral districts.

91

This "strange journey," from Adam Smith's theories of capitalism to the creation of single member districts in San Antonio, Texas was caused not just by all the direct forces of various political actors who migrated to and caused the city to become what it did but it was also affected by other seemingly unrelated forces. For instance, if it had not been for Chinese parents in San Francisco, California, Latinos would have never been accorded coverage under the Voting Rights Act of 1965. Essentially, Lorenz's Butterfly Effect is exemplified by the policy effects resulting from the now famous Lau v Nichols (1974) Supreme Court decision that gave birth to bilingual education for the Chinese-language children of San Francisco. After many political iterations this language protection was extended to Spanish Speaking persons and eventually led to the extension of the Voting Rights Act of 1975. The extension of protection under the Voting Rights Act to Spanish Speakers was used as political leverage to force the City of San Antonio to change its city council electoral system from an at-large configuration to a single member district structure.

It is inconceivable that the political actors surrounding the bringing and arguing of Lau ever imagined that their struggle would lead to the imposition of single-member city council electoral districts in the South Texas city of San Antonio. Yet it did and the public-policy process of San Antonio City Government was irreversibly changed due to the extension of the language rights of Chinese children far away on the West Coast of the United States. In this instance the butterfly's flapping wing had, indeed, caused a "Tornado in Texas."

The state changes form as a result of either its inability to absorb change or just the opposite, its ability to accommodate change. This particular characteristic of the state can be perceived by understanding the state as *a complex matrix of systems, structures, and processes.* The state is structurally changed because this matrix, or some point on or within the matrix, intersects with some variable, an occurrence that may or may not be able to be predicted and/or which may not occur more than once at either regular or irregular intervals. Change occurs at the exact moment of contact and the state's form is changed irreversibly. The rate of change and extensiveness of change, the degree of dissipativeness, is due to the intensity of the effect on the system. As the voting rights example mentioned earlier indicated, the extension of the Voting Rights Act of 1965 to language minorities in 1975 dramatically altered both the configuration of San Antonio's City Council and the manner in which the city government would produce public policy up to and including the present.

The extension of the Voting Rights Act resulted in the creation of single-member city council districts that, in turn, resulted in the council being populated by a significantly larger number of Mexican Americans. As a matter of fact, the 1977 city council elections, the first under single member districts, saw majority control pass into the hands of African and Mexican Americans for the first time since the early 19th Century when electoral power was held almost exclusively by the Mexican community. The other structural effect resulting partially from the electoral structure's change was a restructuring of the local ruling regime as evidenced by the dissolution of the Good Government League (GGL). The GGL was a reform-type political machine that slated candidates for the city council and dominated city elections from the middle of the 1950s through 1975. Because the political system was dynamical and the forces wore the legitimacy of law and were not catastrophic or crisis creating, the San Antonio political system was able to absorb the changes with a minimum of discomfort.

This structural change was caused by more than simply the passage of the VRA and the consequent threat of a civil rights lawsuit. In social systems the bifurcation point that Prigogine spoke of can last for an extended period of time and include the effects of many variables. In the above incident the other major factor which caused a change in the city's governing form was the fact that a struggle had ensued among the city's economic elite for control of the private economy. The struggle was a direct result of a conflict over the developmental philosophy concerning the direction, scope, and pace of both physical and economic growth. Although significant chapters of the struggle went unrecorded and were played out within the confines of the inner sanctums of the private sector, the struggle was manifested in the political arena because economic development philosophies could not be realized without gaining control of the rule making and policy interpretation mechanisms of the city. In short, one must control government, either directly or indirectly, in order to have control over the creation and implementation of a city's economic development policies. Essentially, the business community's support split in the mayoral election of 1980, bringing Henry Cisneros to office and forever relegating the candidates of the GGL, backed by another business group, to the "dust bin of history." Those business leaders who felt that the city's future lay in expansive growth that would eventually link San Antonio to Austin geographically supported Cisneros. Those business leaders who preferred to concentrate developmental efforts in the central city core, on the other hand, supported the GGL.

Both the changes in the political and private arenas of San Antonio, Texas were enabled by, and in turn caused, changes within San Antonio's society. These changes were reflected in the evolving political styles, the governing, electoral, economic, and social structures of the city. A tabular presentation of San Antonio's changing political environment is presented below. The table is a depiction of the evolution of San Antonio's political regimes from approximately 1920 to the present and shows the evolution of the governing and electoral structures of San Antonio during the same time frame. Each typology represents a "structure of authority" that includes not simply the formal governmental arrangement as set forth by Easton (1965) but includes the private sector's decisional processes that drive public policy as well (Lindblom, 1974).

The city-regime typologies depicted in the table were constructed for easier conceptualization and identify effects of the power struggles on various institutions or segments of San Antonio's society. These typologies appear across the tops of both tables together with the approximate dates of their existence. The dates are approximate due to the aperiodic or dynamical nature of the system and the generally accepted notion that one cannot precisely identify a specific

94

occurrence or a specific instance effecting the wholesale restructuring of a social system (Boorstin, 1990).

A dynamical social system's structures evolve gradually and are affected by the almost simultaneous interaction of a multitude of variables or attractors. The timing governing when each variable will interact cannot necessarily be predicted because it depends upon the perceptions of various political actors pursuing their self-interests and/or the narrow interests of their organizations. Generally, these interests, perceptions, and consequent actions are not coordinated always and are not based on a holistic perception of how these actions will affect the greater system. In other words, political actors or public decision-makers when considering various policy options very rarely can or will consider all possible externalities resulting from their specific decision or action. Lindblom points out that this is true because of the human and technological limitations that make gathering and sifting all the information necessary to make a rational decision veritably impossible (1974). On the micro-level, the decisions may appear rational but on the macro-level both the decision and any subsequent outcome may or can be viewed as illogical, contradictory or paradoxical. The resulting effect is unintended change or changes in the political system. This is the strange attractor effect spoken of by chaos theorists. Attractors are variables that are essential, normal parts of a dynamical system. Strange attractors are those unexpected effects arising from the interaction of attractors within the dynamical system. In the case of political systems the strange attractors are the unintended changes resulting from the interaction of a multitude of variables occurring within a bifurcation point or a specific historical period.

Typologies

The typologies in the table reflect the manner in which the local political regime play(ed) politics based upon the regime's perception of its role within the city and its interpretation of "where the city is or should go" in its evolution. "The game of politics" in pre-1948 San Antonio closely resembled how classical political machines manipulated the political processes during Tammany Hall's era

95

of control in New York, Mayor Daley's Chicago, and the White era in Boston (Riordan,

| | TABLE 3-1 | | | |
| | | Regime Typologies | | |
Typologies	Machine City	Reform City	Entrepreneurial City	International City
Years	1915 – 1948	1949 – 1973	1973 – 2001	2001 - ?
Transition Years	1905 – 1917	1941 – 1951	1955 – 1973	1989 - ?
Private Sector Interests	Small Business Saloon Keepers Gamblers	Savings & Loans Local Bankers Lawyers	Local & National Developers State & Regional Banks	National & International Developers Multinational and International Banks
Governing Structures	Commission	Council-Manager	Weak Mayor Council-Manager	Strong Mayor Council Manager City-County Consolidated Government
Electoral	Partisan At-Large	Non-Partisan At-Large, Place	Non-Partisan Single-Member Districts, Mayor At-Large	Non-Partisan Expansion of Single Member Districts Some Councilmembers At-Large[1]

1994; Banfield and Wilson, 1966; and Bridges, 1984). In San Antonio the "Machine Era" began in approximately 1885 and culminated in 1951. Although this appears to be a rather long time it was not without its periods of instability. The machine's instability, which manifested itself with the ousting of the machine between 1899 and 1905 and with tenuous electoral victories until 1914, resulted from the political struggles that occurred within the ranks of the city's private elites.

It is attributed that Bryan Callaghan, Jr. who held the mayoralty from Feb. 1, 1885 through Dec. 5, 1892 when he resigned to take a county judgeship, founded the original machine. In Texas, the county judgeship is similar to the Chair of the County Board of Supervisors in California. Mr. Callaghan gained reelection on Feb. 22, 1897 for one term relinquishing control on Feb. 22, 1899. Between 1899 and 1905 the anti-Machine forces controlled City Hall but Callaghan came back, winning the mayoralty on June 1, 1905 and passing away while in office on July 9, 1912. Bryan Callaghan was the mayor of San Antonio, Texas for 16 1/2 years, the longest tenure of any mayor regardless of historical era. Callaghan maintained his political power base among the German and Mexican immigrant communities and the Mexican American populations together with the working class and small business community. He controlled the local political scene through the traditional machine style by awarding contracts to friends and jobs in local government to those who supported his organization. Nonetheless, Callaghan's machine, because it neglected the interests of the local economic elite, fell to the forces of the early city supporters of the "Reform Movement" then sweeping across the United States (Booth, et al, 1983).

The Machine Era of San Antonio politics did not end with the demise of the Callaghan Machine because the reformers who replaced Callaghan eventually fell prey to the machine-style politics Bryan Callaghan had pioneered. This was due primarily to the fact that many of Callaghan's followers eventually took over the reform organization, at the same time taking over the city government, and

---

[1] These last changes are still in the "talking" and negotiation stages.

organized and ran the local political scene like a machine. The reformers had proposed a commission form of government and a more professionally run government as an alternative to how the traditional machine government had been run. But these plans were laid aside until 1914 when the Callaghan organization was again defeated, this time for good. The subsequent city council elections of 1915 were the first to be conducted under a commission structure that would stay intact for 31 years. Nevertheless, as pointed out by Booth, et al (1983) the Callaghan organization's demise was of its own making. It failed to restructure itself to accommodate the changing demography of the city and it failed to incorporate the reform perceptions of the electorate. Where Callaghan had depended upon a coalition of German and Mexican and Catholic voters the new reformers depended upon Anglo, Baptist voters. Where Callaghan's organization had perceived economic development as being dominated by the local elites of brewers and ethnic entrepreneurs, the reformers based their perception of economic development through the eyes of bankers and real estate developers. By 1919, however, the commission membership was made up not of representatives of the local elite but of saloon keepers and former Callaghan machine politicians. Eventually, the commission form of government allowed each of the commissioners to run their area of responsibility like small "fiefdoms" and again the reform focus was lost. Instead, the commission members began concentrating on maintaining control of city government through patronage. This political situation lasted in San Antonio until 1946 when Mr. Walter McAllister, a local savings and loan executive, founded another reform group named the Council-Manager Association of San Antonio.

The organization founded by McAllister took two years to organize itself enough to challenge the "Commission Ring" electorally as the commission machine was popularly called. In 1948 the new reformers petitioned the mayor, Alfred Callaghan the son of the famous machine mayor, to place a council-manager charter revision initiative before the voters. The mayor refused and he was challenged electoraly by Jack White, a local hotelier and member of the

Council-Manager Association. Mr. White ran as a reform advocate championing the council-manger form of government and proposed a broad array of reforms as essential elements of his campaign platform. Some of Mr. White's platform "planks" included the professionalization of city government, a massive health program to include fumigation, extension of municipal services to newly annexed areas, and an overall upgrade of the city's infrastructure. Although Mr. White beat Mr. Callaghan the other commission members won reelection in 1949. In the subsequent municipal elections of 1951, however, the Council-Manager Association put forth an entire slate of candidates who overwhelmingly beat the remaining commission members. After the election as one of the first items of business before the new city council a charter revision commission was formed and chaired by W. W. McAllister. The commission subsequently put forth a council-manger form of government before the city voters in October of 1951 that passed by better than a two-to-one margin. This initiative victory effectively and officially ushered San Antonio into its Reform Era.

Although, the reform government did bring the city a civil service system which bolstered the professionalization of city services, upgraded infrastructure, expanded health services, and annexed record numbers of miles of land, the political organization controlling the local political process refused to change with the times. The regime that controlled the reform city council changed its name to the Good Government League (GGL) in 1954. Although the GGL was open nominally to the public it became a closed knit group of local savings and loan executives, attorneys, and businessmen. The GGL eventually fell victim to the forces of entropy (Rifkin, 1980) in that it failed to do anything to replenish its membership or its leadership ranks and the organization's agenda-setters refused to allow new ideas, particularly concerning economic development, to be brought forth in San Antonio's political arena (Booth, et al, 1983). Additionally, the GGL leadership also reflected a developmental philosophy that preferred to limit investment initiatives to the defense and tourism sectors that were anchored by the Central Business District (CBD). This philosophy began to come under criticism

99

more and more as a newer group of private-sector leaders wished to expand developmental activities far beyond the CBD and to diversify local economic options. This new group increasingly saw the GGL as a barrier to overcome rather than as a group of compatible businessmen and natural allies.

Compounding the tension within San Antonio's private sector were the political pressures placed on the local governing regime by the passage of the Civil Rights Acts of 1965, specifically the Voting Rights Act (VRA), the agitations of the local Raza Unida Party, the birth of an Industrial Areas Foundation (IAF) community organization called COPS (Communities Organized for Public Services) and a changed local social structure due to the influx of migrants from the Central and Northeastern part of the United States. Because the GGL was not flexible enough to absorb the demands of these various social and political forces it lost the political advantage that it enjoyed within San Antonio's political environment and formerly disbanded in 1976.

Eventually, the departure of the GGL from the political scene left much of the electorate without a traditional signal setting organization. Even though the GGL was criticized more and more as it refused to change, it still provided the electorate with an easily identifiable entity from which they could receive an indication of who or what issue to vote for. The absence of the GGL from the political environment created a fairly chaotic dynamic similar to the one originally envisioned by Robert Dahl when he first spoke of pluralism (1961). But because of the racial antagonism that has always underlain San Antonio politics the types of coalitions essential to a pluralistic environment were not easy to construct. For a number of years, approximately between 1973 through 1981, there were a broad array of independent politicians or small groups of politicians that gained minor political victories over the GGL slates. By 1981, however, regime power was consolidated by the new business community elites who had a broader developmental vision for the city than the GGL's fathers (Flores, 1989).

The new regime supported the mayoral candidacy of Henry Cisneros, who brought with him not merely a charismatic personality but the vast majority of the city's Mexican American voters. The arrival of Mr. Cisneros on the political scene was bolstered by the imposition of single-member city council districts in 1979. San Antonio's city government was "threatened" by a VRA lawsuit by the Federal government's Department of Justice that forced the city to place a single-member district initiative before the voters. The initiative passed winning approval by 51.3% on January 15, 1977. The support for the initiative reflected the sharp racial divisions of the city with the voting precincts heavily populated by Mexican Americans supporting the proposition overwhelmingly. On the other hand, those precincts populated by heavy majorities of Anglos only voted for the proposition at a 28% level. The less heavily segregated sectors of the city supported the proposition at rates that ranged from 52% to 55%. The measure itself passed by only 1673 votes out of more than 64,000 cast (San Antonio, TX, 1977). Nevertheless, in 1979 the city held its first city-council elections under the new representational structure and five Mexican Americans and 1 African American won seats on the ten-person council. For the first time since 1847 persons of color held the majority of seats on San Antonio's governing council (Booth, et al, 1983; Montejano, 1987).

Single-member districts did more than change the manner in which politicians were elected to office and how the citizenry were to be represented, it also changed the style of politics so that a more "free-wheeling," free-market approach to coalition formation and political support best characterized how the local political regime had to approach the manner in which political power was wielded in San Antonio, Texas. Coalitions among the various politicians, representing distinct communities, became the key to controlling the public agenda, insuring that the agenda's goals were achieved (Flores, 1991).

It is generally accepted throughout the community, and reflected in the campaign contribution reports he submitted for each of his mayoral elections, that local developers controlled the city's public agenda during Mr. Cisneros's tenure. Henry Cisneros maintained his control over the city council's decisional process by assisting various Mexican American city council members in their electoral efforts. Additionally, the local and national business communities understood that Mr. Cisneros's developmental philosophy was compatible with theirs. Essentially, Henry Cisneros was, he still is, a Mexican American who happens to also be a "New South Democratic" politician who believes in utilizing economic development as a method of solving many of the social ills befalling society. Mr. Cisneros's developmental philosophy was such that it emphasized encouraging the private sector to pursue investment opportunities as freely as possible within San Antonio, Texas (Flores, 1991). This "free-wheeling" style of politics I have labeled "Entrepreneurial" in that many of the private political players were developers and entrepreneurs who at various times throughout their business careers either made large amounts of money and/or lost large amounts of money through developmental speculation. Whether individual political actors were able to play the game of politics depended upon their economic health. The stability of the coalitions, maintained by Henry Cisneros, were dependent upon the wealth generated by the developers together with the manner in which their activities were sold to the citizenry of San Antonio. Ineffective public relations could and did put an end to some coalitional efforts such as the failed pursuit for surface water reservoirs in the 1990s.

As always, however, times were changing and so was the political landscape and, consequently, so would the face of the political regime and the style in which politics was played in San Antonio. The city's geographical location, it is the largest United States city closest to Mexico's northern industrial heartland. The city's location combined with its unique population, it is approximately 56% Hispanic and has an identifiably prominent Mexican American middle class, places San Antonio in a strategic position to play a significant "bridging" role in any economic, social, or political activities surrounding the implementation of the North American Free Trade Agreement (NAFTA) provisions. Although the vast majority of economic activity generated by NAFTA has bypassed San Antonio for Houston, Dallas, New York, and Miami the Mexican Government has indicated that San Antonio is perceived by both

102

their governmental and business officials as a city which can provide their families with a comfortable cultural setting. The racism and xenophobia, which traditionally has confronted Mexican Americans when interacting with many of the state's public and private institutions, has not been lost on Mexican nationals and government officials. Racism is more subtle and less evident in San Antonio consequently representatives of the Mexican business and governmental communities are making San Antonio their homes and cultural bases and commuting to do business in Dallas and Houston. Data on home ownership and school enrollments is sparse but an interview with the Mexican Consul General in San Antonio has lent some substantiation to this suspicion. Finally, both the United States and Mexican Governments have seen fit to recognize San Antonio's unique niche by locating a principal branch of the North American Development Bank (NADBank) in the city. This bank oversees and plays a significant role in many trans-border investment decisions

The anticipation that NAFTA was going to pass U.S. Congressional scrutiny coupled with increased investments from Great Britain (entertainment) and Japan (microelectronics) has created new players in the development of a political agenda and the style in which San Antonio politics has been played since 1989 and will be played into the next century. In recent years international trade missions, headed by Prince Charles of Great Britain, the late CEO of Sony Corporation, and former and current Mexican Presidents, have visited San Antonio looked to the city government for increased spending on capital improvements particularly those supporting private sector investment opportunities. Although the political style of the regime still reflects an entrepreneurial flair, it is more internationally and growth oriented; consequently, this regime typology has been labeled "International."

Private Interest Sector

Regimes can be defined generally as the "formal ways in which political power is organized and exercised in any society" (Greenberg and Mayer, 1990, p. 14). This organization centers around the manner in which a society is structured, which group sets the rules and standards for that structure, and how various social groups come together to organize political control of the state apparatus. Thus, Stone concluded that "An urban regime may be defined as *the informal arrangements by which public bodies and private interests function together in order to be able to make and carry out governing decisions"* (1989, p. 6). In the case of San Antonio, Texas this requires an understanding of how the city's economic elites have been structured and how this structure has evolved throughout the city's history. Additionally, the linkage between the city's controlling elites and the local government must be operationalized. Finally, the manner in which the various social groupings are incorporated into the governing regime must be identified.

The economic elites, who dominate a city's political regime, arise because of the manner in which the economic system is structured and the partnership between the economic and political systems is developed and nurtured. The private sector elites are elites because they either nominate themselves to play the game of politics; their economic activities are such that they account for a significantly large share of a city's economic foundation; or they have been recognized for having a long history of familial involvement in political, civic, or economic affairs (Dahl, 1961; Hunter, 1953; Lindblom, 1974). The economic elite represents but a small circle of individuals within the private sector and for the most part speaks to their own perception of the manner in which a city should pursue economic development activities. This perception changes from one historical era to another depending upon the state of the national, regional or international economy, technological innovations, and the expectations of the local community.

In the case of San Antonio, Texas the economic elite has been dominated by a combination of individuals representing the foremost organizations from the private sectors that fuel the city's economy. So that at any given time, throughout the history of San Antonio, the economic elite will be composed of a combination of individuals representing established sectors such as banking, ranching, and

104

transportation reinforced periodically by immigrants from other geographical areas of the United States. The contemporary elites of San Antonio reflect this combination yet it is a volatile combination in that not everyone's perception of developmental philosophy changes simultaneously. The faces of the elites change due to many factors including death, economic fortune, or simply in or out migration from the political arena. What is certain after a review of the history of elites in San Antonio from 1835 to the present is that the individuals who have played significant roles in molding the developmental philosophy of the city and also attempted to manipulate the local governmental system in that regard cannot be considered monolithic. Which elites play a dominant political role in the governing regime depends upon the outcome of accommodations and struggles occurring within the business community. As political power is contested publicly, private power is contested privately. The one aspect of the private struggle that remains constant is that the winning group always includes new immigrants and newer generations of existing notables, who enter elite circles with the assistance of some of the older elites. The new elites always appear to require the assistance of some of the older elites who share a developmental philosophy and may be at odds with the remainder of the older elite community. In turn, the winning elites will remain powerful for a significant period of time until they also undergo disagreements among themselves, new players arrive "wanting a piece of the economic pie," or "young turks" emerge wishing to push the old guard aside.

Four types of elite structures specific to San Antonio characterize the principle types of "private interest sectors" which dominated(s) local politics. These are identified in Table 3-1. It appears that what differentiated the sectors principally, from one historical era to another, was differing developmental philosophies. The individual elite actors are not necessarily important in that individuals who occupy these positions sometimes remain the same for decades, sometimes they pass from the scene victims of economic fluctuations, sometimes

105

they leave the community for more fruitful business opportunities, and sometimes they die leaving no descendants interested in playing the game of politics.

What is important to understand is that the manner in which property relations are defined and the manner in which the elites have generated their wealth guarantee the elite's place or role within the social structure. For example, the private-business-sector elites who dominated local politics during the "Reform City" era represented a class of individuals who derived their wealth from local real estate investments based upon their control of local financial institutions, particularly savings and loan associations. The most notable of the individuals during this era was Walter W. McAlister, who made a fortune in the savings and loan industry and was one of the founding members of the Council-Manager Association and the GGL, and eventually winning the mayoralty of San Antonio for a decade. An anecdote one hears reflecting Mr. McAllister's control over city council affairs is that during his tenure as mayor the city council agendas were decided upon and all votes precast in his savings and loan offices, which were located directly across the street from City Hall.

Eventually, the Reform City Elites had to make way for the Entrepreneurial City Elites who, as was pointed out earlier, set forth a different developmental philosophy for the city, supported the candidacy of Henry Cisneros, and managed to manipulate the large Mexican American electorate to counter the machinations of the GGL. Like Mayor McAllister before him, Mr. Cisneros reigned for almost a decade uninterrupted by any serious political competition. During his tenure Cisneros was politically and financially supported by the younger developers' campaign contributions.

The interesting aspects of Table 3-1 are those areas labeled as Transition Periods located between the various typologies. These areas demarcate what in Chaos Theory are called "bifurcation points" or points where a system faces a crossroads between chaos and stability (Kellert, 1993). Which road the system takes is dependent upon how the system reacts to the forces affecting it at the time. If the system absorbs the effects of the force(s) (generally there are a broad

106

array of forces coming to bear on a social system) then the system tends toward stability, absorbing the effects and changing its structure(s). In the long run this results in an evolutionary process that will give birth to a system that will look dramatically different over a long period of time. If the system refuses to absorb the forces then the system becomes more and more chaotic until it is forced into a stable phase or passes out of existence. This is generally what occurs when a political system is forced into a revolutionary situation as a result of its inflexibility. It will pass out of existence and another dramatically different system will replace the old. In San Antonio politics the "bifurcation points" covered varying numbers of years when several incidents (forces) occurred, both within and without the community. These forces effected the change from one regime type to another changing from Machine, to Reform, to Entrepreneurial, to International.

For example, the change from a Reform to Entrepreneurial regime type was effected by seven different social and political occurrences coming to bear on the community between the late 1960s and the early half of the 1970s. These forces or pressures on San Antonio's dynamical political system changed the structures that, in their entirety constitute the public policy decisional processes of the city.

1. A telephone rate-increase scandal involving several GGL city councilmembers;

2. A public utility rate-increase "scandal" where the GGL-dominated city council voted for one level of increase and the citizens were forced to pay exorbitantly higher rates than what had been advertised;

3. The local Chamber of Commerce had been placed on an annual one million-dollar retainer by the GGL dominated city council without the citizens being made aware of the contract;

4. The Industrial Areas Foundation-based Communities Organized for Public Services (COPS) was founded on the west and south sides of the city

107

giving low-income Mexican American neighborhoods a powerful voice in local and state politics;

5. The Raza Unida Party won control of Crystal City Independent School District, Zavala County, and the Crystal City Council ninety miles to the south of San Antonio unleashing xenophobic fears of "Mexicans taking over everything in sight;"

6. The Federal Government's Department of Justice threatened a law suit against the city government if they refused to consider changing electoral structures from at-large to single-member districts; and,

7. The "split" among the business community over developmental philosophies.

The GGL struggled mightily to maintain control over the city government amidst all of this turmoil but eventually lost total control of the electoral process by 1979 when independent Hispanics and African Americans won an electoral majority on the council. Between 1955 and 1971 the GGL's electoral control had been so complete that they had won 77 of 81 contested city council elections an astounding 95% victory rate,. Between 1973 and 1977, although the GGL still managed to win seats on the city council they lost majority control and the mayoralty. The GGL formally disbanded as an organization in 1976. The GGL's demise was self-induced because it refused to upgrade its public policy agenda to conform to the changing times, it did not recruit new membership or nurture new leaders, and it failed to change its magisterial style to interact with the more activist Chicano community of the 1970s. In short, the GGL and its leaders became overly inclusive and inflexible ideologically and philosophically. Its inability to incorporate or manage the forces of chaos caused the GGL to pass from San Antonio's political scene. And, the GGL's passage from San Antonio's political scene removed an institutional signal, a referent if you will, for the city's electorate; a signal indicating the saliency of candidates and/or issues.

Governing and Electoral Structures

As Stone (1989) pointed out, the second half of the urban regime consists of what comprises the "public bodies." Unlike Stone, however, I feel that, like the private-interest structures, those of the public bodies also change over time[3]. In the case of San Antonio, the changes to the political structures occurred within the same approximate timeframe as those of the private interest structures. Two political structures, "Governing" and "Electoral," have been chosen for discussion here and their changes are depicted in Table 3-1.

"Governing Structures" are defined as the type of structures, adopted by a city's charter, which determine and/or define the relationships between elected officials, bureaucrats, and citizens. As depicted in Table 3-1, San Antonio, Texas has had four different types of "Governing Structures" since 1915. Between 1915 and 1948 a commission form of government governed the city where the commissioners were elected in partisan elections to positions overseeing various agencies of the city's bureaucracy. Once in office the commissioners used the traditional machine techniques of patronage and graft to solidify their hold over their respective departments and insure their reelections.

Coinciding with the demise of the commission machine, locally dubbed the "Commission Ring," came the rise of the reform organization in 1948 called the "Council-Manager Association," later to become the GGL, this transition ushered in a council-manager form of government. The GGL hailed the council-manager form of government as their principal plank in the mayoral campaign of 1948 that was won by Mr. Jack White. As pointed out earlier, a charter revision election, held in 1951, quickly followed where the citizens adopted the council-manager form of government. An essential aspect of this change was a concomitant change in the electoral and representational structure from a partisan to a non-partisan, at-large, place system. In other words candidates would not be allowed to use a political party banner under which to run, all city council candidates would run throughout the city as opposed to standing for election in a specific ward or district, and each candidate would file for a "numbered place" on

---

[3] Stone appears to feel that structures must be rigid constructs which cannot undergo substantive changes but can only experience changes on the margins (pp. 9-10).

the ballot. The place itself meant nothing except that it became traditional during the hey-day of GGL control that, in various elections, the candidate who filed for either the number 1 or 9 city council place was in actuality running for the mayoralty. How, this particular place designation came about appears to be lost in history. Nevertheless, the change in the governing structure was effected by the changing regime. The changes in the regime structure, in turn, were caused by the inability of the commission machine to efficiently and economically provide a graft and nepotism-free government that also could provide local municipal services efficiently and fairly.

The council-manager form of government remained in place until various sectors of the city's regime, principally the Mexican American and developer elements from the business communities, began voicing their discontent with the distribution and quality of municipal services and the developmental direction that the city was taking respectively. Mexican Americans complained bitterly that the city council, and their "hand-picked" managers, paid scant attention to the needs of the city's east, west, and south sides where the vast majority of Chicanos and African Americans resided. Tensions reached such a high level that a recall initiative was begun in the spring of 1974. The petition did not succeed but the ensuing publicity caused the GGL-backed city council a high degree of embarrassment and added to their already decaying credibility.

As was pointed out earlier, developers who wished to create large-scale subdivisions centered on shopping mall complexes beyond San Antonio's CBD split with the old-line business community who wished to limit developmental activities to the central city area. This younger group of developers felt that the GGL-controlled city government was not planning, nor would it, with the expansion of the city in mind. Expanding the city's land space, for the younger developers, translated into elevating San Antonio into a higher tier of cities nationally. Some of the developers even felt that San Antonio had the potential of expanding north to Austin and as far south as the Mexican border creating one of the largest "megalopolises" in the entire United States. One very young entrepreneur with mayoral ambitions who was politically close to Cisneros spoke of turning San Antonio into a "major league city" with development centered on major professional sports. The older business establishment saw all of this as "pie-in-the sky" rhetoric that would only place undue stress on the city's infrastructure and eventually lead to increasing taxes and an unwanted invasion of immigrants from both the northern part of the United States and south from Mexico.

Underlying the three-way tensions created by the Mexican American community, the developers, and the older business communities was an attack on the electoral system initiated by President Nixon's Justice Department. The GGL's non-partisan, at-large, place electoral system that had been the central plank in their reform platform 25 years earlier was seen as antiquated and in violation of the Voting Rights Act of 1965. Although no lawsuit was litigated, it was filed and quickly settled, the threats and ensuing negotiations resulted in a Special Election to modify the City Charter. The new charter not only included 10 single member districts but a separate mayor's office elected at-large. Although the mayor's office possessed few substantive powers and was mostly ceremonial, the person holding the position was responsible for supervising the weekly city council meetings. As a result, someone with a strong personality or possessed of a great deal of charisma could manipulate and control the city council agenda if they were shrewd politicians, a task that Henry Cisneros found to his liking during his eight-year tenure as mayor.

Although the new mayor's office was weak structurally, there were no legislative powers such as a veto to allow the mayor to "statutorily" influence the passage of laws, the office, if utilized properly, could be used to moderate the conflict expected to arise among the district-based council members. Additionally, the new city manager would be required, for the first time, to have professional academic training in public administration. These structural changes coincided with the eventual disappearance of the GGL from the political scene in 1981.

Between 1981 and 1989 the governing and electoral structures remained stable and did not change. By 1990 a mayor reflecting the changing political dynamics of the city ruled over an uncomfortable, tenuous, and unofficial relationship between the factions making up San Antonio's new regime. Henry Cisneros's charismatic and authoritative leadership style had become the norm for the mayoralty, the city's physical shape had undergone extraordinary changes expanding far beyond the city's traditional limits, and, for the most part, citizens became used to the scene of city council meetings dominated by a significant increase in Mexican American council members. Once the new regime came to power the planning department changed the developmental philosophy of the city moving to annex more and more lands on the fringes of the city allowing for the large building and economic boom of the 1980s and 1990s. The new single member districts allowed the Mexican American communities to elect as many as five of the eleven city council members. This new electoral change also resulted in the businessmen who had won the war of the private sector to champion the causes of relatively independent Mexican American politicians for the first time since the late 1830s.[4]

As the developmental rhetoric changed during the decade of the 1970s it also began to change again in the late 1980s when various factions of the development community began championing the cause of international economic activities. This changing discussion was due to an eventual downturn in the Texas oil industry which had provided much of the capital for the real estate activities of the 1980s. The decline in oil prices led to an almost total collapse of the development community. After "the dust settled" those who remained began looking for other types of investment activities besides real estate. Many began looking at initiatives possible under the new, proposed North American Free Trade Agreement (NAFTA).

---

[4] Mexican Americans who had run during the GGL era were chosen through the secretive "slating process" utilized to choose their city council candidates. These Mexican American candidates were always perceived in the Chicano community as being owned and beholden to the old, aristcratic, and racist "gringos" who controlled the life of the city.

Assisting in this latter situation was San Antonio's already important place in Mexico's history. Many persons not familiar with San Antonio's history simply understand the city's place as the home of the Alamo an image which has become part of America's psyche because of the immortalization by Hollywood. San Antonio, however, was and is much more to Mexicans. At one time in the history of Mexico, San Antonio was the northern-most colonial outpost for both Spain and later Mexico. Throughout Mexico's tumultuous 19th and early 20th Centuries' history San Antonio provided a political haven for many of Mexico's exiled political and intellectual elites from Porfirio Díaz to Jose Vaconsuelos to the Flores-Magón brothers. Díaz was Mexico's President during its initial 20th Century industrialization and modernization period. Vasconsuelos was one of Mexico's leading intellectuals of the 1910 Revolution and eventually helped to democratize and revolutionize Mexico's public educational system. The Flores-Magón brothers were revolutionary journalists and theorists prior to the 1910 Mexican Revolution who influenced many of the earliest revolutionaries. After the Mexican Revolution of 1910 and the consolidation of political power by the *Partido Revolutionario Insitutional* (PRI) San Antonio became a center of cultural contact for Mexicans with the United States. So that to the Mexican and United States governments, it would appear that San Antonio would be a perfect conduit for trade and communication between the two countries. This was substantiated partially with the establishment of a major branch of the North American Development Bank in 1992.

The Dynamical State and Chicano Empowerment

Although the dynamic nature of the state allows it to change from one historical era to another it also creates the conditions under which political power changes hands from one political regime to another. An essential element of the transition of power for groups generally considered politically powerless or having a very low capacity for influencing politics at the local level is that this particular historical bifurcation point is when these same groups can ascend to political power. Essentially, the transition period during which political power is

113

transferred from one political regime to another is the time when the local political regime is at its weakest. As a result, this transitory period is also the same time during which the "best" conditions for Chicanos exist, or other political out groups, to gain access to political regimes. A review of the structural machinations surrounding the period during which Henry Cisneros came to power as the Mayor of San Antonio, Texas is sufficient to illustrate this proposition.

Henry Cisneros required the support of both the Chicano community, organizationally represented by COPS, and the business community to win and maintain electoral control over the mayoralty. The imposition of single member city council districts, the changing of private power within the business community, and the increased political efficacy of the Mexican American community exemplified by the intense organizational activities of COPS all served as catalysts for the weakening of the power hold of the dominant regime. This resulted in a relative power transfer from one political regime to another. Consequently, this also marked the first time since the 1830s when the local Latino community held a significant amount of influence over the local state. Nevertheless, because the essential nature of the state is founded in a capitalist economic system it would still create and implement public policies that nurtured the inequality endemic to the Chicano community. This state dependency is the direct result of the close nexus between the public and private sector nurtured within liberal democracies mentioned in an earlier chapter. The next chapter will provide an example of how the public/private nexus intensifies the social inequality of Latinos in San Antonio.

Chapter Four

The Social-Political Inequality of Latinos

and the

State Structure

Both the dynamical nature of the state and the manner in which the state is structured creates barriers against the social and political empowerment of Latinos. The political or electoral barriers are more flexible and subject to more change, as opposed to barriers that exist in the private sector, because by definition they are accessible to the general public. In a democratic society the citizenry possesses the ability to participate and change the fundamental electoral structures of that society. On a fundamental level, change can be effected through the election of officials that change or rearrange the public agenda or petitioning elected officials to create new or different policy options from those already in existence. On another level, the various participatory efforts by citizens are reflective of continuous power struggles that occur over control of the local state apparatus by specific political actors or organizations. Although these struggles are designed essentially to effect and redirect the public policy agenda they also redefine or reconstruct the state apparatus. Political participation then results in political and electoral structures changing form, from one historical era to another. On the other hand, private sector structures remain somewhat inflexible and closed to the participation of the vast majority of the public simply because they

115

belong to the private sector. The changes they experience are also due to power struggles among contending groups representing different factions of the business community as described in the previous chapter. The nexus between the public and private sectors allows for what Rosales (1999) has characterized as the "Illusion of Inclusion" because the participation in the electoral process creates the impression that the broader polity is participating in an open and democratic process. On the other hand, the closed nature of the private sector's decisional processes and structures prevents the broader society from participating in those institutions having control over the economic wellbeing of one's everyday life.

Although participation in the electoral processes appears easy, and oftentimes is, its dynamic and flexible nature presents one with a duo-faceted situation. In the first instance, because the electoral process lies in the public realm it is accessible to "out groups" or those groups, such as Latinos, who have been excluded from participation historically. Nevertheless, access is not easily gained; oftentimes, access can only be brought about through either political organization/agitation and/or through appealing to the courts for redress. After access is gained, however, it is often the case that other forces, again either internal or external to the state, react to manipulate the structure in such a way as to make access difficult once again. This notion is reflected in the historical struggle over the electoral processes and structures of San Antonio's city council. The "new, reactive" change tends to minimize the access requiring the "out groups" to press forward demanding additional reforms. The evolution of the electoral structures, then, is the result of a constant struggle between the "outgroups" wanting inclusion and forces, generally representing business interests or the dominant regime (Stone,1989; Bridges, 1998), not wanting to allow the "outgroups" easy access.

This chapter has possesses two sections that discuss the political power struggles in San Antonio, Texas. The first, discusses both the closed nature of San Antonio's economic development process and its effects on the city's social structure highlighting the biased nature of the decisional process. The second

116

section discusses the city's electoral process in order to point out the manner in which Latinos are continuously excluded from that process through the constant structuring and restructuring of the electoral processes. Electoral control is also hampered by the intense racial polarization of the electorate that has left many able Latinos from winning seats on the city council. This latter situation was changed, however, due to the threatened Voting Rights lawsuit of 1975. Nevertheless, without the court's intervention representatives of the Latino community have traditionally been prohibited from easily accessing the public facet of the city's economic development processes.

Part One

Economic Development in San Antonio, Texas

Although the dynamical nature of the state creates conditions where Chicanos can gain a political "foothold" in the governing political regime by winning some elections, simple electoral victory does little, if anything, to alleviate the social inequality that normally afflicts the Latino community. The principle reason for this is that the fundamental structural relationship between the public and private sectors, which dictates the direction of a significant amount of public policy, is the principal factor determining the Latino community's place within America's social structure. The state's reliance on the private sector for the generation of revenues in order to provide essential public and municipal services coupled with the fact that the private sector provides for the basic well-being of everyone in a liberal democratic society, generally places the interests of the private sector over those of the Latino community. Generally, this structural arrangement places the controlling level of the economic development decisional process out of direct reach of locally elected officials. The power equation, at least in the economic development realm, places control of the decisional processes and structures firmly in the hands of private sector elites. The dominance of the private sector's interests in the public policy process creates the conditions for the public/private nexus. Most importantly, the private/public nexus becomes the central economic development principle permeating the rhetoric of all political actors within society including bureaucrats, politicians, and

118

the average citizen. Essentially, the public/private nexus directs the ideological orientation of the community. This ideological orientation acts as more than just "social cement" holding the society together it "qualifies individuals for social action." Essentially, ideology goads individuals to act in a particular manner. In the public policy process this translates into the creation and implementation of public policies that serve the dominant interests of liberal democracy—the private sector.

The contention that the state structure produces policies that create and/or exacerbate the social inequality of Chicanos will be explored through a detailed discussion of the decisional processes that give birth to the general economic development policies of San Antonio, Texas. Not only will the processes be probed but the ideological orientation of the policies will also be discussed in great detail. The most important aspect of this discussion is that during the time frames presented here San Antonio had elected a Chicano mayor who had conducted his campaign with the promise that the vigorous pursuit of economic development policies would go far to alleviate the poverty and blight of the city's racial minority communities. Although one cannot, nor should one ever, generalize from a case study this is one example where it is assumed that if a community elects a mayor of color he or she can significantly provide relief for the poverty experienced by minority communities. Nevertheless, the liberal democratic state structure militates against any efforts that minority mayors, or city council members for that matter, might pursue to improve the social well being of Chicano communities.

Before proceeding with the substantive discussion concerning economic development in San Antonio a cautionary note regarding these data is in order. Unlike many "big city" planning departments, San Antonio's Planning Department does not maintain construction or socio-economic status data by community planning units or city council districts. Why this situation exists is not clear. Secondly, San Antonio's political culture, which mirrors the state's, is one which is based on the notion that the "best government is one that governs least"

119

(Davidson, 1990). As a result, the city's planning function, like many of its other functions including some of the "necessary services" such as police and fire protection, is kept to a minimum. Data gathering is performed situationally rather than as an ongoing enterprise. Rather than using data to monitor and systematically plan for the use of land, data is used to substantiate public policy decisions. This sort of planning orientation together with the size of the city is reflected in the small size of its planning bureaucracy. Where most large cities have separate divisions for Long Range, Specific, and Community Planning, San Antonio has individual planners responsible for these activities all working within the same division.

The only economic development activities performed by San Antonio City Government are maintaining an inventory of land use characteristics and ongoing activities intended to attract industries to the city. These latter efforts include the creation of a "one stop" permit process, initiated during the first days of the Cisneros Administration in 1981, and maintenance, of a labor pool characteristic information bank by the city's Department of Economic and Employment Development. The city planners and various other agencies concerned with economic development base their projections strictly on U.S. Bureau of the Census tract information specifically generated for a given situation. This is unlike, for example, Los Angeles that possesses a bureau, Planning Research Section of the Systems and Mapping Division of the City Planning Department, responsible for generating demographics for use by both the elected and bureaucratic officials. If any San Antonio city council person wishes to obtain any demographic data concerning a specific policy issue within their district they must do so on their own initiative using their own or donated resources. For example, it was discovered, in 1987 by Councilwoman Maria Berriozabal, the first Chicana elected to the city council in the city's history, and who represented an inner city district heavily populated by Chicanos, that San Antonio did not possess an appropriate housing inventory upon which to launch a low income housing study. An unpaid graduate student intern compiled a city wide housing inventory for Ms.

Berriozabal as part of a Master's Thesis project. These data were then used as the baseline information for a housing needs assessment for Ms. Berriozabal's district.

San Antonio's and Texas' libertarian political culture (Lemare, 1998) notwithstanding, another reason explaining the minimalist approach to the planning process may reflect the active efforts by the private sector, specifically the development community, to capture political control of the city's planning functions during the mid-1970s. For instance, the development community first made their intentions public for the intensive development in the northern part of the city by the creation of a "Northside Expressway." Specifically, developers wanted a freeway extension connecting the Central Business District (CBD) with the geographical area due north of the city and above Interstate 410. This freeway extension could then link the central business district where many residents worked and tourists resided to a location where the construction of a "supermall" was being contemplated. The developer's plan drew vociferous objections immediately from both the Mexican American and environmentalist communities.

Many of the objections were fueled unintentionally by a group of recently hired "progressive" urban planners concerned about the environmental consequences of development in the northern portions of the city. The principle concern, articulated primarily by the Aquifer Protection Association (APA), a private group of environmental activists, was based on the fact that San Antonio's "sole source of drinking water," the Edwards Underground Aquifer, laid directly beneath the proposed mall development. The aquifer, which is a sophisticated series of limestone caverns of unknown dimensions, is also geologically and ecologically very fragile. The situation is compounded by the fact that the aquifer is replenished only by rain water falling on the "recharge zone" which lies in the Texas Hill Country immediately north of and in the northern portions of the city. Essentially, the argument from the environmental perspective was that development over the aquifer would cover up much of the porous surface through which the rain water filtered into the caverns. As a result both the geological and hydrological integrity of the aquifer would be endangered by development of the

121

mall.. Additionally, environmentalists argued that threatening the geological integrity of the aquifer would also threaten the integrity of several flora and fauna species protected under the federal Endangered Species Act. As a result, a lawsuit was filed, by the local chapter of the Sierra Club, and development over the aquifer was placed under scrutiny and control of the federal courts. This insured that only controlled development occurred on and around the aquifer's boundaries. State and local governments were forced to submit plans that balanced environmental with developmental concerns. Nevertheless, the court's decision as to whether a developmental plan met appropriate standards was based upon "reasonable" recommendations by the submitting jurisdiction. In short, the court would not interfere unless it appeared that the development substantially threatened the aquifer's ecological integrity and the local elected body approved the development. Although development over the aquifer appeared controlled it was, and is, still subject to the political machinations of developers and their supporters because of the court's reliance on the local jurisdiction's approval. This is so because of the dependent relationship that has evolved between developers and the elected officials of San Antonio.

The environmental concerns were compounded by the economic concerns of the Chicano community. Acting as the Chicano community's representative, COPS voiced objection that the continuing developmental activity to the north would place considerable economic strain on the availability of jobs and consumer goods for low income persons. The debate became so heated that it resulted in a close city council vote, 6 to 4, in June of 1977 to prevent development over the aquifer. This decision was overturned, on a subsequent appeal from the business community to individual council members approximately six months later, that opened the developmental floodgates.

The resulting developmental explosion can be demonstrated partially by the dramatic population growth experienced by the northern half of the city over the next 18 years. For example from 1980 through 1995 fully 88% of all residential construction occurred in the northern half of San Antonio. United

States Bureau of the Census data reveal that the population growth during the same time frame mirrors the construction rate in that it increased by 80% while that of the southern half only grew 2.6%. So that fully 96% of San Antonio's population increases over the last 18-25 years has occurred in the northern portion of the city.

While the debate between the developers and the Chicanos and environmentalists raged, a loosely organized group of developers decided that the San Antonio Planning Department had become infused with planners who were not ideologically or philosophically compatible with visions of unlimited and uncontrolled growth. The developers' group maneuvered to get one of their own, Mr. Ralph Bender, appointed president of the city's Planning Commission which oversaw the Planning Department. By 1980 the developer led and dominated Planning Commission engineered the rescission of the controlled growth, pro-environmental General Plan and replaced it with no plan at all. So that between 1977 and 1994, when work began on a new General Plan, the city operated *sans* plan(s). This is particularly important since the political machination negating the city's planning functions also occurred during the approximate same time frame that the city experienced its most intense developmental and population growths. Eventually, the developers forced out all but one of the "young, progressive planners" who had created the pro-environmental General Plan from the Planning Department. Some of the planners were co-opted in the classical sense, becoming employees of the same developers who were responsible for their firing, other planners simply found employment in other cities, while still others went into private consulting in San Antonio. This political struggle, much of which went unnoticed by the local populace, became known locally as "The Developer Wars" (Casey, 1985). In the end, the wars left the city of San Antonio with no planning function during the high growth decade of the 1980s which, as will become evident in a moment, tended to intensify the social and economic segregation the city had experienced for decades.

Essentially, in the city business interests have dominated both the economic development and political processes from the turn of the 20th Century to the present as was outlined earlier. Private sector hegemony over economic development planning has been particularly intense since San Antonio's Reform Era began in 1951. The growth and investment patterns have occurred generally in those geographical areas possessing higher income and land values (Booth, et al, 1983, p. 48; Flores, 1989). These growth patterns are characterized by rapid population expansion and the proliferation of commercial districts in the northwest, north central, and northeast geographical sectors of the city and away from the west, south, and east sides of the city. Table 4 –1 reflects the general population growth of San Antonio between 1970 and 1995 by geographical region.

San Antonio's Mexican American community resides primarily on the south side of the city and county of Bexar. The population shifts between 1970 and 1995 have been dramatic in that the share of the population residing within the northside of the county grew from 54.7%% in 1970 to 69% in 1995. The share of the population living in the southern part of the county dropped from 45.3% to 31%

during the same time frame. This dramatic population shift is depicted in Table 4-1 and emphasizes that the growth in the northern part of the county coincided with a loss of population in the southern tier. The increase of inhabitants predicted for 1995 over the 1990 numbers is based upon new electrical connections reported by the local utility company, City Public Service Board, as opposed to the data for

124

Table 4 – 1			
San Antonio Population Growth Patterns			
by			
Geographical Region			
1970 - 2000*			
Year	**Northside (%Δ)** **(%Share)**	**Southside (%Δ)** **(%Share)**	**Total (%Δ)**
1970	454,539 (54.7%)	375,925 (45.3%)	830,464
1980	608,048 (25.3%) (61.5%)	380,740 (1.3%) (38.5%)	988,788 (16.1%)
1990	806,662 (24.4%) (68%)	378,802 (-.5%) (32%)	1,185,464 (16.6%)
1995	893,462 (9.7%) (69%)	400,689 (5.5%) (31%)	1,294,151 (8.4%)
2000	N/A	N/A	1,392,931 (14.9%) α

1970, 1980, and 1990 which were taken from U.S. Bureau of the Census reports. Preliminary population counts by the United States Bureau of the Census indicate that the population trends evinced in Table 4-1 have continued. The general population growth rate for the county was 16.1% from 1970 to 1980, 16.6% between 1980 and 1990, and 14.9% between 1990 and 2000. The data on construction activities throughout the county indicate that the population shifts from the southern to the northern tier of the county continue.

The population growth figures coincide with the increase in construction activity occurring within the same general geographical areas as exemplified by

---

* **Source:** United States Bureau of the Census Reports, 1970, 1980, 1990, and 2000.
α Percent change calculated between 1990 and 2000. Percent change between 1995 and 2000 was 7.1%

the construction of new single family dwellings. As Table 4 - 2 indicates between 1980 and 1994 the

Table 4-2*

Single Family Residential
Development in Bexar County
1980-1994

Property Tax Accounts (Parcels)

Year	Northern Tier	Southern Tier
1980	121,150 (47.2%)	135,580 (52.8%)
1985	147,250 (49.8%)	148,289 (50.2%)
1990	157,580 (55.8%)	124,682 (44.2%)
1994	176,674 (56.4%)	136,706 (43.6%)
2000	222,315 (58.7%)	156,169 (41.3%)

Average Value
Single Family Residential Accounts

1980	$73,206.72	$30,656.16
1985	$80,402.68	$30,620.13
1990	$83,334.82	$35,803.67
1994	$88,375.77	$31,850.22
2000	$99,215.87	$44,269.12

Source: San Antonio, TX. Bexar Appraisal District. "Schools: State 'Self' Reports." 1982, 1985, 1990, 1994.

share of single family dwellings has increased from less than 50% in 1980 to 58.7% in 2000 for the northern tier of Bexar County. The value of the property has also continuously increased. The average value for a single family dwelling in the northern tier of the county went from approximately $75,000 in 1980 to $99,215.87 in 2000. On the other hand, the average value for a single family

---

* Table 4-2 is the same as Table 2-1.

126

dwelling in the southern half of the county went from $30,656.16 in 1980 to $44,269.12 in 2000. The interesting aspect of the data at Table 4 - 2 is that the property values show a steady and continuous increase for those homes in the northern tier while the values of those homes in the southern tier appear to fluctuate. The difference in housing values, which have stayed relatively stable over the twenty year period covered in Table 4-2, points out that a sharp economic difference exists between the value of housing in the north and the value of housing in the southern tier of the city.

Commercial development has proliferated in the northern tier similarly to single family housing. The increased commercial development is portrayed in Table 4 - 3. The data indicate that of commercial development has increased continuously in the northern

tier of the county while the share enjoyed by the southern tier appears to steadily decrease. In 1985 there were 5195 commercial property tax accounts (each account represents a single parcel of property designated as being commercially developed) which represented 37.2% of all commercial development within the northern tier of the county. The total taxable value equaled $4,396,896,610 for an average value of $846,370.86 per parcel. By 2000, commercial development in the north accounted for 44.7% of all having a total value of $6,739,551,881 for an average value of $899,326.38 per parcel. The data for the southern tier reveal that although it still retained the majority of commercially developed property the total value was consistently half that of the northern tier while the average value per parcel was significantly less than those parcels in the north. The commercial development activities include a variety of construction projects including shopping malls, commercial shopping strips, and individual retail outlets. The extreme difference in the values between the northern and southern tiers of the county reflect the scope of the developmental activity that exists in either tier. In other words, the property with higher values generally represents large scale development such as shopping malls while lower valued commercial development generally represents smaller types of retail activities such as convenience outlets

127

or traditional "mom and pop" stores of the type that normally proliferate throughout inner cities.

Table 4-3

Commercial Development

Accounts and Property Values
(nonadjusted dollars)

Northern Tier

Year	No. of Accounts	Avg. Value	Total Value
1980*			
1985	5195 (37.2%)	$846,370.86	$4,396,896,610
1990	6464 (40.6%)	$702,640.70	$4,541,869,503
1995	6630 (42.3%)	$626,410.63	$4,153,102,462
2000	7494 (44.7%)	$899,326.38	$6,739,551,881

Southern Tier

Year	No. of Accounts	Avg. Value	Total Value
1980*			
1985	8765 (62.8%)	$326,981.27	$2,865,990,864
1990	9466 (59.4%)	$270,728.53	$2,562,716,252
1995	9045 (57.7%)	$248,772.96	$2,250,151,435
2000	9287 (55.3%)	$327,158.84	$3,038,324,157

*These data were included with industrial parcels for this accounting year.
Source: San Antonio, TX. Bexar Appraisal District. "Schools: State 'Self' Reports." 1982, 1985, 1990, 1994.

Booth and his colleagues concluded that the manner in which "developers, bankers, insurance men, and physicians from northern San Antonio" create a type of prioritization system directs the economic development growth patterns by allowing investors to make their decisions based upon general market force

128

indicators or personal opinions. For example, developers have conceded that they plan development in the northern half of the city because that "is where things seem to work well," "that is where everything is happening," and "that is where everyone wants to go." These comments along with similar perceptions were gathered during a series of confidential interviews conducted with various of the city's active developers between 1987 and 1990. One developer was candid enough to point out that the primary reason for the lack of development in the southern part of the city was because that was where the low income community resided. Consequently, there was little wealth that could be spent on moderately or highly priced housing or consumer products. As a result, the low income areas of San Antonio were not areas for fruitful investment. Additionally, he pointed out that these areas were more risky than others because one could not control the uncertainty surrounding one's investment. Compounding the risk was the effect of the high crime endemic to the low income areas of the city. High crime rates, particularly property crime, have a tendency of intimidating potential investors. Although these interviews were open-ended and did not represent a statistically significant sample of all possible San Antonio developers, these anecdotes seem to represent the general perception of the development community given the population growth patterns reviewed.

Additional data substantiating the developers' perceptions indicate that 86% of all industrial parks, accounting for 78% of all available acreage set aside for that specific use, are located in the northwest, north central, and northeast sections of San Antonio (Greater San Antonio Chamber of Commerce, 1986). By 1990 these percentages had increased to 89% and 81% respectively with an additional 38,000 square feet planned for 1991 in the North Central sector of the city (Greater San Antonio Chamber of Commerce, 1989). In 1985, six of eight regional shopping malls together with all six of the new proposed malls existed within or were planned for construction in the three northern sectors. By 1989 an additional two malls had been constructed, one located in the CBD, Rivercenter which caters principally to tourists; the other, Rolling Oaks Mall is located on the city's far north side. The two additional malls already under construction, La Cantera and Shavano Park, lie to the extreme northwest in areas where rather affluent housing is constructed and, much to the dismay of local environmentalists, directly over the Edwards Underground Aquifer. Additionally, there are conceptual plans for three more "outdoor malls" for various parts of what has now become known as "The Greater Northwest" part of the city.

Table 4-4

San Antonio Regional Shopping Malls

Existing Malls	Square Footage
Fiesta International (Near Westside)	Demolished 1991
Central Park (North Central)	650,000
Ingram Park (Northwest)	1,153,000
McCreless (Southeast)	460,000
North Star (North Central)	1,200,000
South Park (South Central)	650,000
Westlake Mercado (Northwest)	450,000
Windsor Park (Northeast)	1,123,000
Crossroads (Northwest)	650,000
Rivercenter (CBD)	1,000,000
Rolling Oaks (North Central)	100,000
Proposed Malls	
La Cantera (Northwest)	600,000
Shavano Park (Northwest)	1,000,000

Source: San Antonio, TX. The Greater San Antonio Chamber of Commerce. "Economic Indicators." 1994.

Of the two malls that were constructed in areas having significant Chicano populations only one, South Park Mall, can compete on a square footage basis (see Table 4-4). The other retail mall, Fiesta International Plaza, experienced

130

severe economic problems due to a lack of business and closed in 1990. Fiesta International comprised only 250,000 square feet of space, which was extremely small compared to the other regional malls and would have made it unattractive to a retailer large enough to anchor a mall of significant activity. Nonetheless, one of Mayor Cisneros's final objectives while in office was to encourage both private and public sectors to think of ways in which to utilize the "ill-fated' mall. To allow the failure of Fiesta International without "lifting a finger" would be sending the business community false signals concerning the city government's commitment toward an unlimited growth philosophy. Unlimited economic development and growth as a way to insure the economic health of the city was the cornerstone of Henry Cisneros's political philosophy and it endeared him to the younger business leaders of San Antonio and guaranteed their continual support in his mayoral campaigns. The support of developers also proved essential to the election of Ed Garza in the 2001 mayoral elections. Both local public and private sector officials feared that a lack of effort on the part of the mayor might have frightened away future economic development investments. By the beginning of 1991, however, Fiesta International Mall stood as an empty landmark to the city's commitment to a lassez-faire planning philosophy. Eventually the physical structure was razed and by 1995 only an empty lot existed where Fiesta International once stood. Nevertheless, the state did come to San Antonio's rescue because construction was scheduled to begin in early 1996 on a downtown "extension campus" of the University of Texas at San Antonio (UTSA). Final construction was achieved in 2001. As an aside the main campus of UTSA is constructed in the far northwest of San Antonio relatively proximate to the proposed La Cantera mall.

Two other indicators that land use patterns will continue to the north, away from where the vast majority of the Chicano community resides are where office space and residential construction have proliferated recently. Fully 70% of all existing office space lies in the northern half of the city. As of 1985, 29 percent of the office space lay in the CBD "a decrease from 1982, when 33% of the total

131

existing office space was located downtown" (Ricecenter, 1985). Office space on the southside decreased from 1.7% of the market in 1982 to .9% as of January 1985. The prognosis is that "the market for San Antonio office space is expected to grow steadily over the next few years, given the city's aggressive business development program, competitive land and construction costs, and the available labor pool. This growth is likely to occur across all eight office activity centers" (Ricecenter, 1985). It should be noted that all eight office activity centers, with the exception of the CBD, are located in the northern half of the city far from the Mexican American community. Finally, as of 1999 all nine planned office projects were completed on the northside and two of the three scheduled for completion in 2000 were also sited on the northside.

Finally, as with industrial and commercial land use the majority of single family residential construction is also located in the northern half of the city. "This pattern is due to San Antonio's historic direction of growth and the location of employment centers" (Ricecenter, 1985). Data indicate that between 1980 and 1995 fully 83% of all new single family residential construction has occurred in the same northern geographical growth areas of San Antonio. Additionally, the data on population changes, Table 4-1, indicate that between 1970 and 1995 approximately 80% of the city's growth has occurred in the northern half of the city as compared to a 2.6% population increase in the southern half of the city. Essentially, the overall growth patterns in both land use and population over the last 25 years appear to indicate that developers, bankers, and financiers are insuring developmental patterns that have resulted, and will continue to do so, in uneven development throughout San Antonio.

The implications of the above data are clear in that as property is developed the value of the land increases, on the other hand, land that remains completely undeveloped, especially older inner city residential areas, appears to experience minimal, if any increases in land values. Coincidentally with the uneven development, San Antonio appears to have experienced its equivalent of "white flight" in that all census tracts as of 1980, except five, possessing more than 60% of an Anglo population lie in the northern growth areas of the city. In these growth areas the median family incomes were $21,111.47 and the median values of owner occupied housing were $59,598.30 (San Antonio, Texas, 1984). These figures are in stark contrast to the census tracts populated by 60% Chicanos where the median family income was $8,873.89 and the median value of owner-occupied housing was $20,955.56 (San Antonio, Texas, 1984). These latter census tracts all fall within Interstate 410 and lie within the southern half of the San Antonio.

There are two significant facets to these growth patterns. Fundamentally, the decisions which resulted in the growth patterns were made by representatives of business interests who controlled the local political and governmental processes (Booth, et al, 1983). Secondly, and most importantly to this discussion, is the fact that the geographical areas experiencing little or no growth possess significant proportions of the city's Chicano population. Additionally, as this population has become more concentrated the differences between the income levels of those census tracts possessing high concentrations of Hispanics and high concentrations of Anglos have become wider. For instance, the data at Table 4-5 show the median incomes of those census tracts possessing 60%+ Hispanic and Anglo populations for the decades 1970, 1980, and 1990. The data are categorized by decile percentages of Hispanic and Anglo populations beginning at the 60% level of density. The data indicate that the higher the Hispanic population density the lower the median family income. Conversely, the higher the Anglo population density the higher the median family income. This pattern appears consistent throughout the three decades. Additionally, the growth rates of the incomes have slowed for Hispanics, from 51% between 1970 and 1980 dropping to 39% between 1980 and 1990, as compared to that of Anglos whose median income grew at a 54% rate between 1970 and 1980 and 52% between 1980 and 1990. The differential median growth rate has resulted in an ever widening income difference of 39% in 1970, 41% in 1980 and 53% in 1990. So that it appears that

Table 4-5

San Antonio, TX
Median Incomes of Hispanic and Anglo Populations
in
Census Tracts With 60%+ Racial Densities

Year	60-69% Hispanic-Anglo	70-79% Hispanic-Anglo	80-89% Hispanic-Anglo	90-100% Hispanic-Anglo
1970	$6304.54 7406.54	$6225.30 9759.95	$6193.00 11024.32	$5232.26 10775.73
1980	13108.86 15711.36	12875.47 20258.04	12121.65 22853.79	10572.58 26750.41
1990	22057.59 34396.59	20789.40 34840.45	18834.26 51036.67	17577.75 56383.83

Median Incomes
by
Decade by Race (60%+ Census Tracts)

Year	% Hispanic	Growth Rate	% Anglo	Growth Rate	%Diff Median Income
1970	$5988.78	---	$9741.63	---	39%
1980	12169.64	51%	21393.40	54%	41%
1990	19814.75	39%	44164.36	52%	53%

Sources: United States Department of Commerce. Bureau of the Census. "Census Reports." 1970, 1980, 1990.

median incomes of Anglos and Hispanics, although both are growing, have not been growing at equal rates. This has led to the creation of two communities who are growing further and further apart from each other economically and socially.

There also appears to be an increasing number of census tracts having higher densities of both Anglos and Hispanics. For instance, in 1970 174 census tracts possessed 60%+ of either Anglos or Chicanos, in 1980 this number had increased to 220 and by 1990 300 census tracts had more than 60%+ Anglo or Hispanic populations. At the bottom of Table 4-6 it is clear that there are more

134

census tracts having 60%+ Anglo rather than Hispanic populations. Additionally, the percentage of census tracts possessing 60%+ Anglo or Hispanic populations has remained relatively unchanged since 1970. In 1970 81% of all census tracts possessed either a 60%+ Anglo or Hispanic population. This percentage grew to 83% in 1980 and decreased slightly to 78% by 1990. It appears from this latter data that San Antonio is and has remained a significantly segregated community where Anglos live in Anglo enclaves and Hispanics live in Hispanic census tracts. Although the 60% "cutoff" chosen for the data displays in Tables 4-5 and 4-6 is arbitrary, it does allow one to detect an overall trend in these data. It appears that if one compares the data in the two tables one also finds that the higher the density of Hispanics in a census tract the lower the income while the converse is true for Anglos. In other words, the higher the density of Anglos the higher the income. In the overall scheme of things it appears, then, that the Anglos of San Antonio appear to be reaping more of the benefits of the city's economic development policies than Chicanos. And, as they reap more of the benefits, as indicated by their growing income levels, they also tend to remove themselves from the Hispanic community.

Ideology and Political Power in Land Use Planning

Land use decisions which directly affect the economic productivity, employment levels, and the quality of life provisions of certain communities are those which facilitate commercial and/or industrial development activities. In a liberal democratic society this translates into the dictum that the land use decision making process must necessarily be guided by and be based upon capitalist developmental principles. These principles are embedded within the decisional process through the choice of variables used in the creation of land use policies. The process is also tempered or constrained by two intractable variables--the effects of past development activity and the ideological perceptions of the decisionmakers.

135

Table 4-6

San Antonio, TX

60%+ Anglo and Hispanic Population Density
by
Census Tract

Year	60-69% Hisp	60-69% Anglo	70-79% Hisp	70-79% Anglo	80-89% Hisp	80-89% Anglo	90-100% Hisp	90-100% Anglo	Totals Hisp	Totals Anglo
1970	13	12	10	20	8	22	19	70	50	124
1980	14	14	15	29	17	67	24	40	70	150
1990	22	46	21	60	23	79	32	17	98	202
Totals	49	72	46	109	48	168	75	127	218	476

60%+ Anglo and Hispanic Census Tracts
Totals and Ratio to City Total

Year	Total 60%+Hispanic	Total 60%+ Anglo	Total 60%+A & H	Total Citywide	% Citywide Totals
1970	50	124	174	214	81%
1980	70	150	220	265	83%
1990	98	202	300	383	78%

Source: United States Department of Commerce. Bureau of the Census. "Census Reports."
1970, 1980, 1990.

Influence over a land use decision's substance can take many forms and identifying where within the decisional process influence will be exercised can be a difficult task because of the fluid nature of the process. If one examines the various forms that political power can take, however, some conclusions can be reached concerning the ideological substance and the degree of influence on that substance a specific type of power has. For instance, the power exerted by the presence of existing large scale industrial or commercial activity is never given sufficient weight or consideration. The physical structures that accompany industrial and commercial activity are considered by planners as relatively permanent and must be treated as assumptions in any future planning endeavors. As a result, the power exercised by past planning activities can exert a significant amount of influence over a land use plan's substance.

The influence ideology can exert during the decision making process is extremely difficult to assess, nonetheless this type of power carries tremendous weight far into the future. The very nature of the basic economy of the United States generally and San Antonio specifically dictates that the vast majority of public policy decisions, particularly land use decisions, must be capitalistically oriented. Capitalism per se although an economic system is also the conceptual anchor from which individual decision makers define social, political, and economic reality. Consequently, when pondering public policy alternatives decision makers define a given economic activity in capitalist terms. For example, when attempting to solve an unemployment problem, public decision makers normally turn to the private sector first for a permanent solution. Only as a last resort will the government be seen as a primary employer or capital investor and then the public solution is deemed only temporary. For the most part, the private sector is always turned to for the provision of permanent solutions to social or economic problems. Only in extreme circumstances is a permanent answer sought from the government even when the private sector provides shoddy, inexpensive, or inefficient solutions to problems. Solutions for energy related problems are usually sought from private oil companies or corporations.

Likewise when a local government wishes to improve its general economic environment it will do so through the creation of a "partnership" with the private sector. In San Antonio the liberal democratic principle of creating a partnership between the public and private sectors in order to pursue economic development was, is and will most probably remain a cornerstone of the city's general developmental philosophy. In this instance the public sector lends the private sector the cloak of legitimacy and the sanction of laws, through the passage of "plans" as city ordinances, while the private sector provides the investment capital required to achieve the desired developmental scope and direction.

Part II

The Dynamical Nature of Political and Electoral Structures

The dynamical nature of the liberal democratic state is one of its single most important structural characteristics. This fluid and porous structure allows the dominant groups and classes to maintain control while at the same time insuring that those not in power remain in their subordinate political positions. There is no denying that all groups and classes within a liberal democratic state are continuously contending for power within every possible political arena. Nor, is my contention designed to deny that the acquisition of political power is impossible for "outgroups." As the examples that will be presented shortly depict, "outgroups" are able to win some political struggles and do gain positions of influence within and throughout the liberal democratic state. The best evidence for this assertion is the increased numbers of Hispanic elected officials throughout the United States since 1974. As the data in Table 4-7 indicates since 1974 the number of Hispanic elected officials throughout the United States has increased dramatically.

In 1973 there were 1,280 Hispanic elected officials in Arizona, California, Florida, New Mexico, New York, and Texas, all states possessing relatively significant Hispanic populations. As Table 4-7 indicates, by 1984 these same states showed an increase of 54.2% in the number of Hispanic elected

140

Table 4 – 7

Hispanic Elected Officials by Selected States, 1984 – 1993

State	Year									
	1984	1985	1986	1987	1988	1989	1990	1991	1992	1993
Percent Change										
Arizona	241	230	232	248	237	268	272	283	303	350
45.2%										
California	460	451	450	466	466	580	572	617	682	797
73.3%										
Colorado	175	167	177	167	157	208	192	213	207	204
16.6%										
Florida	44	45	45	48	50	62	63	60	66	68
54.5%										
Illinois	25	26	26	28	28	41	36	40	42	47
88.0%										
New Jersey	12	25	29	34	44	53	45	42	40	44
266.7%										
New Mexico	556	580	588	577	595	647	687	672	688	661
18.9%										
New York	65	63	69	68	68	71	78	76	91	93
43.1%										
Texas	1427	1447	1466	1572	1611	1693	1920	1969	1995	2030
42.3%										

Source: NALEAO, "1993 National Roster of Hispanic Elected Officials," 1993.

officials for a total of 2,794. This increase in Hispanic elected officials continued so that by 1993 there were 3,999 in the same states representing an increase of 30.1%. Interestingly enough the growth of Hispanic elected officials in the remainder of the United States grew from 353 in 1985 to 1, 171 in 1993 an increase of 69.86%. In other words, the rate of increase in the number of elected officials has slowed, although still increasing, in the states reported in Table 4-7, while the rate of increase in the unreported states has doubled. The National Association of Latino Elected and Appointed Officials (NAELO) attributes the increases in Hispanic elected officials to both increases in the Hispanic population in all regions of the country and the implementation of reforms engendered by the Voting Rights Act (V.R.A. of 1965, Pub.L. No. 89-110, 79 Stat. 445 (codified as amended at 42 U.S.C. §§ 1971, 1973 to 1973bb-1 (1988)). One can also add that the increased Hispanic electoral successes have led to increasing levels of political efficacy among Hispanic voters.

It should be noted that the increases in Hispanic elected officials have occurred primarily at the local political levels in municipalities and school boards where more than 3,000 Hispanics were elected in 1993. According to NAELO, in 1993 there were 4420 Latino elected officials throughout the entire United States. Of these 3604 or 81.5% were elected from local or special jurisdictions such as school boards. Only 18.5% of Latino officials were elected to statewide offices in any of the states. This is due partially to the geographical concentrations of Hispanics in certain regions of those states where Latinos are principally located and also the segregated settlement patterns of cities such as San Antonio, Texas. Ongoing Hispanic electoral success at the local level, then, is a logical conclusion. One can also speculate that, mathematically, Latinos can have a significant impact in those jurisdictions where they are a small percentage of the total electorate but sufficiently large to be the difference, the "swing-vote," in some elections between conservatives and liberals or persons of other races, such as Anglos and African Americans (DeSipio, 1996).

The increased numbers of Hispanic elected officials nationally, however, tend to mystify the tendency of the state to create "structural barriers" to the continuing political advances and participation of Latinos. These barriers take the form of additional structural impediments that arise making electoral success more and more difficult over time. Structural barriers arise from time-to-time in liberal democratic states insuring that any possible changes in the governing political power arrangements can be controlled. These barriers insure that new and potentially "radical" ideas and/or persons are prevented from "substantively" challenging the political status quo (Flores, 1988). Sometimes these barriers are consciously created and maintained to insure that political incorporation progresses at a pace that prevents large-scale political change. At other times the structural barriers look like subconscious community reactions to Latino electoral empowerment that occur in cities and towns where Hispanics are politically efficacious and have "track records" of successfully challenging the existing political regime. Such a situation exists in many cities and towns in Texas. Here, however, the situation of San Antonio will provide the case study for a discussion of this phenomenon.

Most of the large increases in Hispanic elected officials have occurred in Texas and many of these increases have been attributed to the implementation of single member electoral districts throughout many cities and school districts. Prior to the implementation of single member districts many local officials were elected under a type of at-large configuration where no residency or representational requirements existed. In many of these jurisdictions Hispanics found it difficult, if not impossible, to elect Latinos to office. After the Supreme Court ruled in White v Register_, 412 US 55 (1973) and after the Voting Rights Act was extended to language minorities in 1975 litigation on the part of Mexican and African Americans increased throughout Texas. Both the Senate Hearings, preceding the VRA's extension, and the court's opinion recognized that multi-member or at-large electoral structures, under certain circumstances, "diluted" both the Hispanic and African American vote. The particular circumstances, according to the court, depended upon the jurisdiction in question and were determined by the degree and intensity of racial discrimination that had occurred historically in those communities. In some communities where Hispanics are the overwhelming majority of the population, such as Laredo, Texas where the Latino population approaches 90%, it is conceivable that the courts may not see at-large election systems as dilutive. The shear number of Mexican American voters always insured that a majority of elected officials were of Mexican descent. As a matter of fact between 1978 and 1993 only Hispanics won city council elections in Laredo. In other jurisdictions, where the Mexican American population represented a significant minority or a bare majority, the courts found that multimember or at-large districts had a dilutive effect. In other words, the at-large or multimember electoral structure tended to enhance the power of the non-Hispanic, Anglo vote while diminishing the power of the Latino voters. The

143

principle reasons were the racially polarized electorate and the refusal of Anglos to "crossover" and vote for minority candidates. Consequently, the determination of whether multimember districts created a structurally discriminatory barrier for Latino voters in Texas was left for the courts to determine on a case by case basis.

Other historical considerations which were identified in the Senate Hearings and specifically identified in Zimmer v McKeithen, 485 F. 2d 1297 (5th Cir. 1973) included everything from overt acts of racial discrimination to discrimination's historical effects, generally expressed through socio-economic data. For example, in many smaller Texas towns and cities Latino children were educated in "Mexican Schools" (Montejano, 1986). In some communities the actual structures can still be identified by local residents and were still in operation as late as 1965. In other communities most of the social institutions were or are still racially segregated. For instance, there were, and still are, Spanish speaking churches as opposed to English speaking churches of the same denomination, Mexican nightclubs and Anglo nightclubs, and the cemeteries are still segregated. In other communities, generally in West and East Texas one still finds active chapters of the Ku Klux Klan who attempt to intimidate local Mexican and African American communities. As recently as 1996 there were Ku Klux Klan rallies in San Antonio and Kerrville, Texas (approximately 45 minutes northwest of San Antonio) that proved to be the beginning of vigorous Klan recruiting efforts. Additionally, white supremacist organizations such as militia and Christian Identity are active both in San Antonio and the surrounding communities to the north and northwest.

Many cities, including Houston, Dallas, and San Antonio, have had a history of police brutality against their Hispanic communities and economic intimidation was and is not uncommon. This last situation generally includes silent boycotts executed against Latino businesspersons when they decide to be vocal about some political or social inequality. Economic intimidation is more common in the smaller towns where "everyone knows each other" than in larger cities. Although in San Antonio it is not unusual for economic intimidation to occur within many sectors including the legal community. Finally, there has always been the xenophobic fear that eventually Mexicans would take over the local political system. In Voting Rights lawsuits this xenophobia is expressed in higher voter turn out rates among Anglos whenever Hispanics threaten to become successful electoraly. In other words in some Texas communities the voter turnout increases whenever it appears that a Hispanic candidate has a chance to win a specific election, on other occasions the turnout is generally much lower. The racially polarized electorate appears to be the product of the decades of racial animosity and intimidation by Anglos and public and private institutions that has been documented by Montejano (1986). This latter situation, combined with multimember districts, is what causes the dilution of the Latino vote. Replacing multimember districts with single member districts, where a jurisdiction is apportioned on a population ratio and where candidates only have to run for election from within the confines of that district, has been the court mandated solution wherever the Hispanic vote has been diluted.

Term Limits as a Structural Barrier

Where Latinos have gained control or at least have made electoral headway, for instance in San Antonio where the at-large configuration has been replaced with single member districts, other structural modifications have been created that weaken Latino voting power. After 1977 when Mexican Americans became political mainstays on the San Antonio City Council a movement began among conservative Anglo voters to place restrictions on the number of terms an individual could hold on the city council. In San Antonio a city council person served for a single two-year term, however, after 1993 all council persons were limited to two, two-year terms after which they were banned from ever holding an elected city office. A city council person, however, upon completion of their two terms could run for the mayor's office. So, unless that candidate possessed the charisma and organizational skills of a Henry Cisneros or was an Anglo they did not stand a chance of winning a citywide election and thus were relegated to serving only four years on the city council. As a matter of fact Mr. Cisneros was

145

the first, and has been the last, Latino to hold the mayor's office since 1847. Historically, the inability of the Latino community to elect a Hispanic mayor has been attributed to the racially polarized nature of the electorate. This trend, however, may have been broken with the election of Ed Garza as mayor in 2001. On the other hand, one election is not necessarily a "trend breaker" and given the facts that Garza was supported by the business community and his Anglo opponent was viewed poorly throughout the city may have explained more why Garza won this election rather than Anglo voters suddenly deciding to vote more willingly for a Latino candidate. Nevertheless, other Latino mayoral candidates would have to win elections handily in the future if the Garza election is to be considered a "new direction" in the electoral behavior of San Antonio's voters.

The arguments surrounding the passage of the term limitation ordinance primarily centered on the notion that incumbents could not easily be removed through the normal electoral process. The ordinance's proponents argued that incumbents had unusually high reelection rates and could only be replaced because of some unusual set of circumstances such as scandal or voluntary resignation. No real data substantiating this claim were ever proffered; nevertheless, an extremely conservative politico to support passage of term limits raised the issue. In the end the voters passed term limitations. The Hispanic community did not support "term limits" but their turnout numbers were so low that they could not defeat the very large Anglo turn out which overwhelmingly supported the initiative.

Later, a Federal lawsuit was filed by Ms. Helen Dutmer, a long time former city council member, who contended that the term limits ordinance violated the Voting Rights Act by denying her Hispanic constituents an opportunity to vote for a candidate of their choice (herself). The court decided, in 1996, that because Ms. Dutmer was a "white woman" she did not have the protection of the Voting Rights Act (VRA) and therefore lacked standing before the court. If the federal challenge to the term limits ordinance had been brought by a Latino plaintiff, the court may have ruled differently. The 'Expert Report"

146

accompanying Ms. Dutmer's petition highlighted two very important aspects of the electoral behavior of San Antonians. In the first place, the report emphasized the racially polarized nature of the electorate--the fact that Latinos and Anglos vote differently from each other and do not tend to support candidates of the opposite race. Secondly, the report pointed out the fact that fewer Latinos actually run, in proportion to their numbers in the city's population, than Anglos. In other words, the actual pool of Latino candidates is much smaller than the pool of available Anglo candidates. In the final analysis, the report concluded that term limits diluted the voting strength of Latinos and therefore violated Section 2 of the Federal Voting Rights Act. A more detailed discussion of the effects of tem limits on the Latino electorate will be presented later in this chapter.

City/County Consolidation as a Structural Barrier

Another effort to further minimize the power of the Mexican American vote occurred through the attempt to consolidate the city and county governments in San Antonio. Representatives of almost all of the city's chambers of commerce together with the local council of governments and the major corporations and businesses of the city populated the "commission" that oversaw the consolidation effort. Many of the commission membership were well known local Anglo politicos who had been involved in local politics for decades. The commission was composed of 26 persons of which only 6 were Hispanics in a community that is 56% Mexican American ("Report of the Voting Rights Advisory Committee on City County Consolidation," August, 1996, p. 6.). A subcommittee composed of academics and attorneys, chosen from the San Antonio community, who were all "experts" or specialists in voting rights law were charged with looking at the effect of consolidation on the voting rights of the local Hispanic community. The subcommittee concluded that consolidation would violate Section 5 of the Federal Voting Rights Act by diluting the Mexican American vote and recommended that consolidation not be pursued. The subcommittee's conclusion was based on the fact that although the majority of San Antonio city's population was Latino, that of the county was not. So that combining the populations of the city and the county would reduce the Latino population to a numerical minority. This could have possibly created the situation where Latinos would lose majority control in any representational electoral scheme created to govern the consolidated government[1]. The commission membership, however, ignored the subcommittee's recommendation and continued to pursue a strategy to insure implementation of consolidation. Their next step was to attempt to place the consolidation issue on the local ballot which required the state legislature's approval for a statewide referendum and rest their strategy on a vigorous media campaign that would play on the heavily racially polarized San Antonio and Bexar County voters. A local Mexican American state senator, Frank Madla, who agreed with the subcommittee's report and killed the referendum effort in the state senate, stopped this movement.

Elimination of Section 5 Coverage as a Structural Barrier

The next assault on the voting rights of Hispanics came in 1997, led by the Republican Secretary of State, Mr. Antonio "Tony" Garza who stated that, since racial discrimination had been overcome in the state, the provisions of Section 5 of the Voting Rights Act were no longer applicable. He recommended that the state petition the Department of Justice to remove Texas from coverage of this provision. Section 5 is a regulatory check where any state political jurisdiction, under coverage of the VRA, that conducts an election and wishes to institute some change to the existing electoral procedures or processes must submit that change to the Justice Department's Civil Rights Division prior to implementation. This is to insure that the recommended changes do not create a retrogressive electoral situation for Latinos or African Americans. Essentially, Section 5 of the Voting Rights Act points out that any change to the electoral structure cannot diminish the electoral gains the minority communities have achieved since the previous change, a change generally ordered by the courts. Mr. Garza felt that given the advancements that Texas has made in the realm of voting rights for Hispanics and the *much improved environment of race relations* (emphasis mine) the Section 5

---

[1] The 2000 Census counts have reversed this situation so that Latinos are now the majority in both the city and county relegating the subcommittee's arguments moot. There is speculation that

requirements no longer applied. As will be shown in the following section of this chapter, Mr. Garza's contention "flew in the face" of political reality given the racially polarized nature of state's electorate generally and that of San Antonio specifically.

What Does All This Mean?

Before delving into the empirical evidence underlying the introductory comments they should be placed in some theoretical context. The brief examples presented so far were set forth quickly in order to illustrate, albeit superficially, that political forces are always moving, applying pressure to build and rebuild structural barriers wherever there appears to be some advancement on the part of "out-groups." In this case, it appears that whenever Latinos have made electoral advancements in San Antonio, Texas efforts were put forth to hinder or prohibit further success. After multi-member electoral districts were changed to make it easier for Mexican Americans to elect Latinos to the city council, term limits were instituted that tended to weaken the powers of sitting councilpersons. With the threat to term limits on the horizon, principally because of the lifetime ban, city/county consolidation arose to further place access to city council seats further out of the reach of Hispanics. And, it appeared that to insure that "if all else fails" the State of Texas was willing to remove itself from the scrutiny of the Federal Government as far as voting rights was concerned.

The above scenario gives one a brief picture of how the local liberal democratic state's electoral structure constantly changes to accommodate those in power. This dynamic property of the state allows for the creation of structural barriers that must be overcome by Mexican Americans in order to have the opportunity to achieve an appropriate amount of representation on the San Antonio City Council. All that remains is to present the empirical data that led to the creation of the above scenario. What follows are discussions of the data that led to the creation and maintenance of single member districts in San Antonio, Texas. This is followed by discussions of the data that support the contention that

---

city/county consolidation will be revisited in the near future and the civil rights community has indicated that they will not object but will cooperate in consolidation effort.

term limits further dilutes the Hispanic vote. Finally, a presentation will be made of the data that city/county consolidation would place effective representation out of reach of Latinos.

Mexican American Turn Out and Racial Polarization in San Antonio, Texas

The principal reasons that multimember districts have a tendency of diluting the voting power of Mexican Americans is that Mexican Americans tend to vote or turn out at lower percentages than Anglos in San Antonio. This is fortified by the fact that the city's electorate is racially polarized. This results in the inability of credible Hispanic candidates from winning a citywide election in a city where Latinos are the majority of the population. Those unfamiliar with San Antonio's demographics might argue that Hispanics generally have a lower citizenship rate than Anglos due to the city's proximity to Mexico and this significantly contributes to the lower participatory rates. San Antonio, however, is the exception to this rule because between 80 and 90% of the city's Latinos are citizens. The cause for the traditional low turnout is difficult to explain in that turnout generally is attributed to a myriad of variables and reasons. For instance, conventional scholarship has concluded that turnout is dependent upon one's educational levels, is related to one's occupation and income levels, and one's family socialization. Traditional scholarship generally has concluded that the more educated, higher income, and professionally employed persons tend to vote at higher rates than individuals in other social categories (Wolfinger and Rosenstone, 1980).

The data on the political socialization of Latinos is still being mined, however, DeSipio (1997) contends that the early exclusion of Hispanics from traditional electoral politics has created a group of "nonparticipators." Essentially, DeSipio's position is that, since neither major political party ever recruited Hispanics and ever incorporated them into the political processes, they have not been appropriately politically educated. As a result, some Latinos, specifically Mexican Americans, have not developed a participatory ethos and, consequently, do not feel that they have a stake in the electoral process. The lack of a "participatory ethos" results in a certain percentage of Latinos not voting. Most importantly, DeSipio feels that this attitude has been passed down to younger generations creating an entire cohort of nonvoters among Hispanics. Taking DeSipio's perception one step further one can speculate that those Hispanics who immigrated into the United States were also subjected to specific political stimuli in their country of origin causing them to define their "political place" a certain way. Immigrants brought this self-definition with them into the United States and it has become an essential element in that individual's socialization. In short, the immigrant transfers her perception of her ability to influence a political structure from one society to another. So, if one was made to feel politically powerless in one country they may very well feel the same in another country and vice-versa.

On the other hand some new immigrants may arrive in the United States expecting to be able to fully participate in their new country, nevertheless, it seems that this expectation must be met by a society that welcomes and encourages the political participation of the new immigrants. This has not been the case, however, in liberal democracies generally and specifically in the United States. DeSipio does point out that European immigrants, at the turn of the century, were welcomed politically by the urban political machines that used the immigrants to bolster their political power. Nevertheless, the state addressed this political "problem" by passing the requirement that only citizens be allowed to vote. Currently, various Hispanic immigrant groups meet differing levels of political acceptance and rejection depending on the local community. Those communities having social organizations designed to integrate immigrants into the greater society tend to bolster the positive expectations of immigrants, while those communities lacking these types of organizations tend to leave immigrants without a positive political support structure (DeSipio, pp. 24-50). Participation rates can be affected additionally by one's exposure to media and the intensity of the media's presentation, the characteristics of the candidate or candidates, the issues brought out during the election, and even the weather on election day.

151

Turnout is also dependent on the strategies of the election, in other words, some candidates will undertake strategies to either increase or depress turnout. This is based on the campaign strategy that a candidate should organize her campaign with an eye toward increasing turnout amongst those voters most likely to support her while, at the same time pursuing strategies to minimize the turnout in those geographical areas that will not support her candidacy. So that "get out the vote" strategies are engineered to increase turnout in only certain areas of the contested jurisdiction while ignoring the electorate in other areas. Last, but by no means least, voting can be affected by the profile of the election itself. If one looks at Mexican American turnout in San Antonio's City Council elections between 1975 and 1997 one finds varying turnout levels, these data are displayed in Table 4-8. As the data indicate, Mexican American turnout averaged 18.2% with a high in 1981 of 55.9% and a low of 6% in 1999. The average turnout for Anglo voters during the same period was 26.8% with a high in 1975 of 43.7% and a low of 7.5% in 1999. As one can see the difference in turnout between Mexican Americans and Anglos during the same time frame averaged approximately 8.6s%. If you removed the Hispanic high of 55.9%, which was Henry Cisneros's fir t mayoral election and was the only time over the last 24 years that Hispanics outvoted Anglos, the average Latino turnout was only 15.1% that increases the average voter turnout difference to 11.7% between Anglos and Hispanics. The presence of Mr. Cisneros on the ballot appears to have galvanized the Hispanic electorate in that during his tenure the difference in turnout between Latinos and Anglos narrowed to 1.4% with Anglos turning out at a 33% rate as opposed to Hispanics who turned out at a 31.7% rate. Without Cisneros on the ballot the turnout difference widened to 15.2% with Anglos turning out at a 30% rate and Hispanics voting at only a 14.7% rate. Essentially, Cisneros's presence on the ballot more than doubled the Hispanic turn out rate while at the same time the Anglo turn out rate only increased 3% during the same time period. Regardless, the increased Latino turnout during the Cisneros years still lagged behind that of Anglos except for one election, his first mayoral election in 1981. Over the entire

152

Table 4-8

Comparison of Hispanic and Anglo Turnout*

San Antonio, Texas

City Council Elections, 1977 – 2001

Year	% Hispanic Turnout Entire City	% Anglo Entire City	% Hispanic Turnout 60%+ Hisp Districts
1977	.127	.265	.30
1979	.188	.319	.214
1981	.559	.377	.631
1983	.159	.215	.181
1985	.255	.364	.268
1987	.293	.365	.218
1989	.088	.250	.087
1991	.228	.382	.238
1993	.122	.313	.143
1995	.085	.210	.087
1997	.094	.220	.10
1999	.06	.075	.06
2001	.111	.125	.157
Means	**.182**	**.268**	**.208**

twenty-two year period of time the only times that Hispanics voted at levels comparable to those of Anglos is when a strong candidate, who could energize the local Latino community, is at the top of the city council ballot.

The presence of a strong Hispanic candidate at the top of the ballot, however, can simultaneously prove to be a "major" difficulty for the Latino electorate. On one level, an attractive Hispanic mayoral candidate tends to drive the Latino vote up. Nonetheless, at the same time the presence of a Henry Cisneros on the ballot also tends to increase the turn out of Anglo voters. As a result, whenever a "credible" or strong Hispanic candidate chooses to run for the mayor's office, Anglo voters tend to vote at higher rates than in those years lacking a Hispanic candidate. This phenomenon appears to be substantiated by the data in Table 4-8. The overall turn out, for the entire city and both groups, was the highest during the years that Mr. Cisneros ran for office (1981, 1983, 1985, and 1987) and again during those years where a "credible" Hispanic candidate ran for the mayor's office (1975 and 1991). Where there is no credible Hispanic candidate the overall turn out rates tend to be much lower. The Garza election in 2001 proved to be the exception to this rule in that both overall turnout and Latino turnout rates remained low. Why this happened has been attributed to the nature of both candidates. Both Mr. Garza and his principal opponent, an Anglo named Bannwolf, lacked charisma, neither excited the electorate either personally or with their position on some issue, and Mr. Bannwolf proved an inept and very unpersonable opponent for Mr. Garza. In a multi-candidate field Mr. Garza garnered 58.6% of all votes cast and carried eight of the ten city council districts losing one northside district by only a few votes. In short, the 2001 election was practically an uncontested election for Mr. Garza. Nonetheless, the historical turn out patterns are consistent with testimony in various VRA law suits throughout South Texas and in all of the jurisdictions of Bexar County that have been sued under the provisions of the VRA. Why Anglo turn out tends to be higher whenever a minority candidate runs for political office is a byproduct, a legacy, if you will, of the racial tensions that have existed in this region for the last 200 years. The high turn out of Anglos is also bolstered by the high degree of racial polarization among Hispanic and Anglo voters during those elections. Racial polarization in San Antonio city council elections will be discussed a little further on in this presentation.

If Hispanic turn out is dependent upon the presence of a strong Latino mayoral candidate during any one election then this dearth of candidates either speaks poorly for the available pool of Hispanic candidates or the enhanced turnout of Anglo voters and their failure to support Latino candidates or both.

---

* San Antonio, Texas, Office of the City Clerk, "Official Returns of City Council Elections, 1977-1997."

Election turnouts, however, cannot simply be explained by the presence of a strong candidate. It is also an artifact of many social, economic, and political variables that, as many VRA cases in and around San Antonio and South Texas have indicated, have framed the political participation of Hispanics in both this city and region. Nevertheless, the turn out pattern where Anglos consistently out vote Hispanics appears consistent throughout the timeframe set forth in Table 4-8 and it can be presumed that this pattern has existed throughout the long history of San Antonio.

To determine which factors appear to have the most influence over Latino turnout, during the twenty two-year period covered in this discussion, regression analysis was used to see whether any other types of structural variables affected turnout rates. The following independent variables were identified: whether the election was held under a single or multimember electoral configuration; whether a "credible" Hispanic mayoral candidate was at the top of the ballot; whether a proposition or initiative was on the ballot; and, whether the election was held under term limitations. The only statistically significant variables that were associated with increased Latino turnout were whether a "credible" Hispanic candidate ran for mayor and whether a proposition was on the ballot. A "credible" Hispanic candidate was one who received at least 15% of the total vote in multiple candidate primaries. These correlations are reported in Table 4-9 below.

Term limitations are closely associated with depressing Latino turnout while a credible Latino candidate is strongly associated with high Hispanic turnout. Whether the election was held having single member districts appears not to have had an effect either way. Although in this data set only one election having single member districts was included. A far better test of this variable would be comparing turnout over an equal number of years. This in itself would be difficult because racial census data by election precinct would have to be gathered for the decades of the 1960s and 1970s.

These data are not available for San Antonio. The earliest demographic data available to use to determine the turnout rates for Hispanic voters is 1980.

155

The effect on Latino turnout of electoral structure type has been the subject of much debate recently. There may, in fact, be a second order effect involved in either increasing or decreasing Latino turnout that has yet to be discussed. It has been demonstrated by NAELO's research that VRA mandated single member districts did increase the number of Latino candidates. And, as the correlations in Table 4-9 appear to indicate, there seems to be a strong and statistically significant relationship between having Hispanic candidates on the ballot and the increase in Latino

turnout. Then one can conclude that single member districts indirectly tend to increase the turnout of Hispanic voters simply because they create conditions encouraging more Hispanics to run for office. Nevertheless, it appears that term limitations would tend to depress the available pool of qualified political candidates generally. As the data in Table 4-9 above indicates, the lowest turn out rates for both Anglos and Hispanics appear in those years where the elections were held under the term limitation rule. Conversely, those years having the highest turnout levels appear to be those where there was a strong Hispanic mayoral candidate on the ballot. On the other hand from 1993 through 1999 the overall turn out rates decrease dramatically. The turnout differential between Anglos and Hispanics, however, appears to remain stable during these elections. As a result one can conclude that either the entire city electorate is quickly losing interest in city elections generally or term limitations is resulting in such a rapid change of political characters that voters are unsure of who they are voting for and, thusly, simply not voting. One can also surmise that voters may feel that since term limits will automatically force elected officials from office they need not participate. The voters, then, are simply conforming to conventional wisdom. When they feel that their vote counts and is worth more, they vote; conversely, when they feel that their vote is not important and is not worth the time required to cast a reasonably rational vote, they will not vote (Wolfinger and Rosenstone, 1980; Teixeira, 1992). Nevertheless, more data concerning term limitations and their effect on the Hispanic electorate will be presented later in this discussion.

156

The other variable that compounds the effect that lower levels of turnout among Latinos inhibits their ability to elect candidates of their choice is the reality that the San Antonio electorate is racially polarized. Racial polarization is the notion that individuals of particular racial or ethnic groups consistently and in higher percentages vote for candidates of their own race. Conversely, these voters do not "cross over" and vote for candidates of other races. This polarization is a reflection of a history of racial discrimination and generally poor

Table 4-9 Hispanic Turnout With Structural Variables

Variables1	Statistics		Hispanic Mayoral Candidate	Percent Hispanic Turnout	Prop Ballot	on Term Limits	MAYOR PCT	Single Member Districts
Hispanic Mayoral Candidate	Correlation Coefficient		1.000	.615	.239	-.408	-.154	-.316
	Sig. (2-tailed)		.	.033	.454	.188	.634	.317
	N		12	12	12	12	12	12
Percent Hispanic Turnout	Correlation Coefficient		.615	1.000	.318	-.641	.210	-.065
	Sig. (2-tailed)		.033	.	.313	.025	.513	.841
	N		12	12	12	12	12	12
Prop on Ballot	Correlation Coefficient		.239	.318	1.000	-.488	.220	.378
	Sig. (2-tailed)		.454	.313	.	.108	.491	.226
	N		12	12	12	12	12	12
Term Limits	Correlation Coefficient		-.408	-.641	-.488	1.000	-.084	.258
	Sig. (2-tailed)		.188	.025	.108	.	.796	.418
	N		12	12	12	12	12	12
MAYOR PCT	Correlation Coefficient		-.154	.210	.220	-.084	1.000	.389
	Sig. (2-tailed)		.634	.513	.491	.796	.	.212
	N		12	12	12	12	12	12
Single Member Districts	Correlation Coefficient		-.316	-.065	.378	.258	.389	1.000
	Sig. (2-tailed)		.317	.841	.226	.418	.212	.
	N		12	12	12	12	12	12

Table 4 - 9 Hispanic Turnout With Structural Variables

* Correlation is significant at the .05 level (2-tailed).

racial relations between groups within a particular community. Racial polarization is measured by estimating the percentage of votes received by a candidate of a particular race by the voters of the same race, throughout the entire city, and comparing it to the percentage of votes received by that same candidate from the voters of other races. The exact level of racial polarization, at least that accepted by the courts, varies from community to community and is weighed on a case by case basis because the degree of racial polarization is affected by a myriad of variables specific to a given city's political history. These variables are outlined by the court in *Zimmer v McKeithen* and range from electoral structures and procedures that were designed to intentionally prevent members of minority groups from voting, such as the memorization of the United States Constitution as a prerequisite to registration, to socio-economic data that reflects a history of discrimination in schooling and in the economy.

Racial polarization in San Antonio, Texas existed prior to 1975 and has remained since. This is evidenced by the percentage of Anglo and Hispanic support received by Hispanic mayoral candidates between 1977 and 2001. As Table 4-10 indicates even Henry Cisneros suffered from the effects of racial polarization. What allowed Mr. Cisneros to continue winning throughout the 1980s were the facts that Hispanics turned out in larger numbers than usual and Anglo voters crossed over to greater degrees than normal. The high turn out and Anglo "cross over" rates, during the Cisneros Years, were underlain by the "political fact" that the Anglo candidates running against Cisneros were not considered strong candidates. This places the Anglo cross over vote in a different perspective in that it is conceivable that if the Anglo community had put forth a strong and attractive Anglo candidate Cisneros's "miraculous run" may not have occurred. Of course, this is mere speculation. Nonetheless, given the historical fact that Cisneros was the only Hispanic mayor between 1842 and 1999 one must remain suspicious as to what the electoral outcome would have been if a strong Anglo candidate had competed against Henry Cisneros during his tenure.

Cisneros's electoral successes notwithstanding, the data in Table 4-10 indicate that during those years where strong Anglo candidates were on the ballot (1975, 1977, 1981, and 1991), the level of Anglo support for the Hispanic mayoral candidates averaged 17.4% while the average Hispanic support for the Hispanic mayoral candidates averaged 72.8%. Conversely, one finds 86.2% of the Anglo voters supporting Anglo candidates while only 28% of the Hispanic voters

Table 4 – 10
Support by Race for
Hispanic Mayoral Candidates
San Antonio, Texas
1975 – 1991

Year	Candidate	Hispanic Support (%)	Anglo Support (%)
1975	Centeno	52.2%	8.4%
1977	San Martin	94.5%	5.5%
1981	Cisneros	72.5%	27.5%
1983	Cisneros	49.9%	50.1%
1985	Cisneros	60.0%	40.0%
1987	Cisneros	64.5%	35.5%
1991	Berriozabal	71.9%	28.1%
2001	Garza	95.9%	53.1%
	Mean	**70.2%**	**31.0%**

"crossed over" and voted for the Anglo mayoral candidates. This high degree of racially polarized voting coupled with the low turn out rates for the Hispanic electorate make it extremely difficult for Latino mayoral candidates to succeed in San Antonio, Texas. One interesting conclusion that can be drawn from the data in Table 4-10 is that Hispanics do "cross over" and vote for Anglo candidates more than the Anglo voters do. This may indicate a number of possibilities. Hispanics may be more tolerant of Anglo candidates than Anglo voters are of Hispanic candidates. Or, Anglo candidates are more acceptable to Hispanic voters than Latino candidates are to Anglo voters. Or, there may be a greater pool of qualified mayoral candidates among Anglo rather than the Hispanic population. Finally it could be some combination of all these reasons. Nevertheless, regardless of what one may make of the data in Table 4-10 one issue is clearly evident. The San Antonio electorate is extremely racially polarized making election to the mayor's office very difficult if not almost impossible for Hispanic candidates.

Term Limitations and Latino Political Participation

The racial polarization of the San Antonio electorate coupled with the low voter turn out rates of Hispanic voters provided some of the rationale for the change to a single member district system with the mayor being the only at-large contest in 1977. The change of the electoral structure from an at-large to a single member configuration resulted in more Hispanics and African Americans being elected to the council than ever before. Theoretically, Latino constituents were able to have their views represented, in any substantive manner, for the first time since 1842. The decade of the 1980s, however, saw increasing agitation among the city's conservative, Anglo community concerning the continuing reelection of an increasing number of Chicano city council members. The principal contention was that it became almost impossible to defeat incumbents. It was also argued that incumbents showed increased tendencies to tender their allegiance to their constituents rather than the wishes of the entire city. Eventually, a "movement" arose attempting to place a "term limitation" referendum before the citizens of San Antonio. Although term limitations come in many varieties, the one proposed for San Antonio carried a particularly stiff penalty. Candidates would be prohibited from running for any other city office for the remainder of their lives, other than the mayor's, after they served two, two-year terms. The proposition was placed on the city primary election ballot in 1991 during the same election where Maria Antonietta Berriozabal challenged Nelson Wolff and the incumbent mayor Lila Cockrell. Another emotionally charged proposition, whether to build a water reservoir on the city's south side, was also on the ballot. Term limitations passed, amidst much publicity and high turn out, and Ms. Berriozabal was forced into a run off election where she was defeated in one of the most highly racially polarized elections in the recent history of the city.

The 1991 Mayoral Election's outcome notwithstanding, the important issue for this discussion is the fact that term limitations passed and became an essential element of the city's charter. Most importantly, however, this electoral limitation became another structural barrier that had to be overcome if Hispanics were to have substantial effect on the city's public policy process. Although one may argue that term limitations tended to suppress the votes of all voters the burden fell more heavily on the Hispanic community for several reasons. First, the lower participation rates among Latino voters became an even more significant factor since these rates appear to have fallen even further than that of the city's Anglo voters during the elections held under term limits (1993, 1995, 1997, 1999 and 2001). Additionally, the term limitation law appears to run counter to the VRA provision that voters in a covered jurisdiction have an opportunity to elect candidates of their choice by denying ballot access to popular incumbents. Term limitations, particularly ones limiting candidates to only two terms in one's lifetime, tend to diminish the pool of available candidates for the Hispanic community. This latter effect of term limitations is particularly insidious given the lower income, educational, and political participatory opportunities for Latinos. Finally, the short tenure imposed by the term limitation ordinance did not allow council members, particularly those with little experience, from gaining enough experience to govern the city effectively. This latter aspect of the term limitation prohibition tended to place more decisional power in the hands of both

161

the city's bureaucracy and the coterie of lobbyists that tends to surround San Antonio City Hall.

Supporters of term limitations argued that the turn over for incumbents was extremely low given the fact that city council candidates could run for reelection indefinitely. The assumption of this argument was that incumbents were susceptible to the control of representatives of various interest groups and tended to disregard the opinions and needs of their constituents. The reality of the situation was that the turnover rate for incumbent city council members was actually lower than the national average. As of 1994 the International City Manager's Association concluded that the national reelection rate for all municipal officials nationally was 83.9% and 84.6% for those cities possessing council-manager forms of government, as does San Antonio (Municipal Yearbook, 1994). Between 1977 and 1991 the overall reelection rate for San Antonio City Council incumbents was 73.75%, well below both national averages.

The effects of term limits have been two-fold on the Hispanic electorate of San Antonio, they have discouraged persons from running for city council office and have suppressed the participation rates of Latinos, even in the single member districts having 60%+ Hispanic registered voters. The data on participation has already been discussed earlier and appear in Tables 4-9 and 4-10 above. The data in Figures 4-1 and 4-2 reveals, however, that the numbers of individuals running for either the mayor's office or one of the district city council seats have diminished since the imposition of term limits. Between 1951 and 1975, before single member districts, an average of 4.1 persons competed for each city council office. Between 1977 and 1991, after single member districts were adopted, the average declined to 3.9 candidates per office. However, between 1993 and 1999, the average number of candidates running for each city council seat fell to 3.3 candidates per office. The candidate per seat ratio is a good measure for determining the number of candidates per office because in 1977 an additional city council seat was added. Prior to 1977, the city had 9 council seats to include

162

the mayor's.[2]   Consequently, the data in Figure 4-2 shows only the candidates
running for city council seats for all elections except those prior to 1977.

Figure 4 - 1

Mayoral Candidates

1951 - 1999

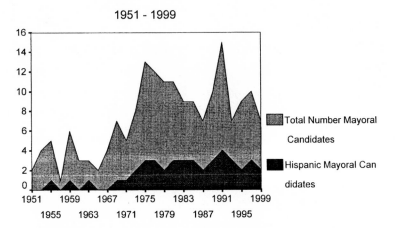

Election Year

Finally, between 1951 and 1977 an average of 4.1 persons competed for
the mayor's office.   Between 1977 and 1991, after single member districts the
number of candidates contending for the mayor's office increased to 7.6 persons
per election.   After term limits, however, the number of mayoral candidates per
election fell to 5.8. As the data indicate, however, throughout the 45 years of data
only one Latino won the mayor's office, Henry Cisneros held the office between
1981 and 1989, and only 37.8% of all 114 candidates were Latino between 1951
and 1999.   Only two African Americans have ever attempted to run for the
mayor's office during this timeframe.   The data indicate an increase of mayoral

---

[2] Prior to 1977 and after 1951 there was no mayor elected directly by the people. Rather, after all
nine council members were elected, they elected a person designated as the mayor from among
themselves. During this timeframe the electoral structure was a "numbered place system." This
was challenged by a VRA suit brought in 1974 and was settled just prior to the 1977 city council
elections. All city council elections subsequent to 1977 elected 10 council members from districts
and one mayor elected at-large.

candidates after the imposition of single member districts and then an immediate decrease after the implementation of term limits. Although the rate of Latinos, running for the mayoralty, increased after single member districts it did not appear to change too dramatically after the arrival of term limitations. The lack of a sufficient percentage of Anglo crossover votes, however, continues preventing Latinos from winning the mayor's office.

The data appear to indicate that term limits, particularly with the lifetime ban restriction, makes running for either the mayor's or any city council office unattractive. Not only are the voters casting ballots in fewer numbers but also candidates are not stepping forward to seek office. An interesting footnote is that this appears to affect both Anglos and Hispanics in San Antonio. The burden, nevertheless, weighs heavier upon the Latino community because, traditionally, they have participated less than Anglo-voters and they have not had the appropriate resources to mount significant political campaigns.

City/County Consolidation and Latino Representation

The effects of city/county consolidation on Latino representation in San Antonio are simple and straight forward and are based on the notion that to pursue this governmental structure, given the racially polarized nature of the city's electorate, is to violate the provisions of the Voting Rights Act. That is, of course, if one cannot find an arithmetic solution to the proportional representation problems that would result if one were to maintain the current number of city council persons.

Essentially, San Antonio, Texas possesses ten city council members elected from districts and a weak mayor elected at-large. There is a residency requirement for all council members except, of course, for the mayor. In other words, in order to represent a district a candidate must reside within the jurisdictional boundaries of the district they intend to represent. As was mentioned earlier there is also a two, two-year term limitation on each city council member with a lifetime ban against running for any city elected office.

164

The city council districts are apportioned every ten years after the census and are drawn so that each possesses approximately the same number of persons. The ratio, as of the 1990 census is 1:93,593. Essentially, each city council district should contain approximately 93,593 persons. The reality, however, is that some districts contain more and others less than the ideal ratio. As a matter of fact, the population figures range from a low of 71,126 in District One to 186,686 in District Eight. District Eight is literally two times larger than District One.

Figure 4-2

City Council Candidates

1951-1999

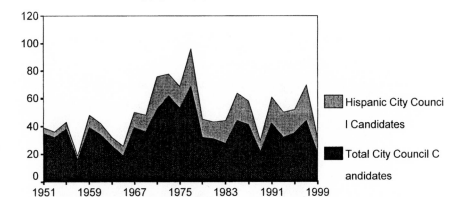

Election Year

These disparities are a reflection of the developmental and growth trends of the city. District Eight lies to the northwest of the city while District One is in the center of the city and encompasses most of the Central Business District.

The principle issue, however, is that under the current configuration and even under the ideal standard six of the single member districts are or would be

165

majority Hispanic districts. The most African American District is District Two and achieved a 44% Black population in 1980 but was reduced to 38.77% in 1990. The racial proportions for each district by race are in Table 4-11. As the data clearly show seven of the ten districts are majority Hispanic, one is majority/minority with African Americans and Hispanics comprising 77+% of the population, and two of the districts are majority "White." The "White category includes Native Americans, Asians, and Others (San Antonio, Texas; Office of the City Clerk, May, 1992). One of the Hispanic majority districts lies in the north, District 9, and is barely 50% Hispanic. This district has never elected a Hispanic council member and is considered a district electoraly dominated by Anglos or Whites. District 2, the majority/minority district, has traditionally elected the sole African American council member. This has become a matter of custom and courtesy in both the city and district. In every election there are "rumblings" among the city's politicos that District 2 may field a competitive Hispanic candidate but to date this has not occurred. All of the Hispanic majority districts with the exception of District 6 have elected Hispanics to office. District 6 has elected both Hispanics and Anglos to office depending upon turnout. Nevertheless, since the inception of single member districts the city's racial minority populations have elected a majority or near majority of the council members.

As the deviations indicate in Column Eight of Table 4-11 the districts are malapportioned. This has been attributed principally, as pointed out earlier, to the migration and settlement patterns caused by the economic development activities in the northern sectors of the city. Most of the development has occurred in Districts 8 and 10 that lie to the northwest and northeast of the city respectively. As the table also indicates this is where the vast majority of the city's Anglo population resides.

As was mentioned earlier, the current single member district configuration was the result of litigation under the VRA and has allowed both the Hispanic and African American communities to elect minority council members. Nevertheless,

166

the decade of the 1990s saw the beginning of discussions, particularly among those business elites who play the game of politics, to consolidate the city and county government. On August 24th, 1995 the city government passed an ordinance creating a City/County Government Commission which was charged with recommending "how the City and the County can better work together under existing laws"; "recommend state legislation to authorize the structural consolidation of the existing City and County government"; and, 'develop and conduct a public education and outreach program to educate the citizens of San Antonio and Bexar County on the advantages and benefits of City-County

Table 4 – 11

San Antonio, Texas

City Council District Population by Race (%)

1980 & 1990

District	1980				1990			
	Hisp	White	Black	Dev.%	Hisp	White	Black	Dev%
1	79.6	15.7	4.7	- .73	83.57	11.86	3.76	-24.01
2	31.0	25.0	44.0	- .41	38.99	20.48	38.77	-20.44
3	44.5	48.4	7.1	+ .54	56.23	33.69	9.3	- 8.78
4	81.7	17.9	.4	+1.7	88.29	10.86	.33	-14.49
5	94.8	4.7	.5	-2.6	94.02	4.37	1.12	-24.78
6	64	28.7	7.3	- .32	75.51	17.64	5.53	-12.54
7	70.4	26.4	3.2	+1.2	77.97	17.7	3.4	- 9.12
8	17	81.5	1.5	+1.4	29.43	64.52	3.7	+99.47
9	37	61	2.0	-1.0	50.09	46.51	2.13	-17.43
10	14.5	82.8	2.7	----	20.35	71.98	5.46	+32.12

Source: San Antonio, Texas. Office of the City Clerk. "City Council Redistricting Information." May, 1992.

Consolidation." (City of San Antonio, Texas; "Ordinance 82692," August 24, 1995)

The ordinance itself appears to indicate that the council intended to encourage the movement toward consolidation and some of the subsequent commission meetings focused partially on the notion of whether this was fact or simply a statement within the charge that was poorly written. Eventually, both the mayor and county judge (the equivalent county official) were queried as to their intent. Again it was not clear other than the commission was to perform background research on which services could be consolidated and what sorts of actions would have to be pursued in order to achieve consolidation (Personal Notes of Commission Meetings, 1996). The ordinance also indicated the composition of the commission. There were to be twenty-six commission members appointed by both the city council, the county government, and jointly between the two governments. On February 20th, 1996 Dr. Henry Flores was appointed to chair the "Commission's Voter Participation Adjunct Committee." This committee was charged with researching "the direction of future county-wide growth patterns and the impact of that growth on the protection of voting rights" (City/County Government Commission, "Letter of Appointment," February 20, 1996).

The Voting Participation Committee (VPC) was populated with academics from Trinity University and the University of Texas at San Antonio and voting rights attorneys from Texas Rural Legal Aid and the Mexican American Legal Defense and Educational Fund (MALDEF). The first indication that friction between the VPC and the Commission was going to occur was when the VPC pointed out that the Commission membership was not reflective of the overall racial composition of the city. The VPC pointed out that 18 of the 26 commission members were White, 6 were Hispanic and 2 were Black. This immediately resulted in a response from the commission pointing out that this was an temporarily appointed group and not a permanent city or county commission that would cease existing once their work was completed. As a result the racial composition of the commission did not have to meet any type of racial

168

composition standard such as reflecting the overall racial characteristics of the city and/or county.

The VPC then performed their charge, under close scrutiny from commission members, and delivered a report that pointed out many difficulties in relation to implementation of city/county consolidation. The principal concern of the VPC was the possible reduction in the concentration of racial minorities as a result of consolidation. The report pointed out that fewer Hispanics resided in the county than in the city and that if the two governments were to be consolidated the "effective reduction in minority population" was "just under six percentage points" from 55.34% (city) to 49.4% under consolidation. This translated into a 10.48% reduction in effective minority population concentration. The report continued pointing out that the United States Justice Department had denied annexations where the Hispanic population had been reduced by as little as 1 and two percent in both San Antonio and Houston previously. The 10.5% reduction was far too high and likely to draw unfavorable consideration from Justice (VPC, "Report of the Voting Rights Advisory Committee on City/County Consolidation," August 1996). The report concluded that the reapportionment required to maintain the current levels of population ratios would require adding at least three additional council districts. As a result, the report added, maintaining the same rough electoral proportions for the Hispanic and Black communities virtually would be impossible. As a matter of record, the VPC indicated that African Americans would most likely lose their representation in any consolidated government.

Needless, to say the commission did not look favorably on the VPC's report and rejected it outright. The VPC chair felt that the commission was intent on pursuing consolidation regardless of what difficulties would have to be overcome and pointed out that the commission risked another VRA law suit if consolidation was achieved. This warning fell on deaf ears! As a result the VPC chair and several of the committee members forwarded their concerns to State Senator Frank Madla, who represented the district having the largest percentage of

Hispanic population in Bexar County. The senator held public hearings on consolidation and used his influence to "kill" the proposed legislation in his Intergovernmental Relations Committee. Nevertheless, the commission members continued to pursue enabling legislation through the state legislature through 1999. At every turn, however, Senator Madla continued to block passage of the legislation.

Another important aspect of this discussion is that three individuals who have been at the forefront of San Antonio politics for over thirty years lead the commission membership. One of the three was a member of the GGL reform machine and the other two were part of the group of businessmen who supported Henry Cisneros in his quest for expanding the city economically. These same individuals were attempting to "push" the city and county governments to expand the scope of local governmental control to encompass the entire county. This, as it was discussed in many of the commission meetings, was necessary for the efficient economic development of the entire northern half of the county. As the data in Part 1 of this chapter point out this would only exacerbate an already uneven developmental picture in the city and further drive a social wedge between Anglos and Latinos in both the city and county. In this respect city/county consolidation would simply be another iteration in the development of the state that would continue to inhibit the empowerment of Latinos within San Antonio, Texas. As far as minority representation was concerned, the Chair of the commission pointed out that the state, regardless of level, was not required to do "anything special" besides insuring that qualified voters were not hindered from participating.

The Conjoining of Developmental and Electoral Politics

The "flexible nature" of the political structures allows them to change in order to minimize the weight of citizens' votes. Bridges, citing a broad range of research, points out that the electoral structures characterizing "reform machine cities," of which San Antonio is one, were designed to minimize political participation particularly by the poor and racial minorities (1997). These characteristics include at-large systems, nonpartisan elections, nonconcurrent election dates, and restrictive or overly stringent registration laws. In some reform cities nonpartisan slating groups (NPSGs) insured control over a specific type of candidate that was malleable to the wishes of the "growth coalitions" dominating the direction of each city's economic development process. This has clearly been the case in San Antonio, Texas. Control of the economic development process is enhanced and legitimized through control of the local electoral system. Under the Good Government League (G.G.L.) this was performed through the secretive slating process where the league, through a series of closed door interviews, selected individuals to run for specific places on the city council. Control by the G.G.L. was generally contested by a loosely organized group of liberal politicians, environmentalists, and representatives of the Latino and African American communities. These contestations, however, proved to be only marginally successful (Sanders, 1975).

In San Antonio the decisional processes and structures are biased in favor of private sector interests because they have a controlling presence on committees or commissions which directly influence both land use and economic development policies. The influence exerted during the decisional processes is not necessarily in the interests of a particular political actor or individual business person rather it serves the general interests of the private sector. So that one sees the faces of private sector representatives changing from one historical era to another due to a number of reasons, such as death or migration, but the private sector itself always finds its appropriate niche within the decisional structure becoming the dominant partner in the governing regime. Consequently, the exercise of political power during the local governmental decisional process includes: (1) the direct efforts by representatives of the business community who create programs to insure a stable investment atmosphere for various companies or corporations of all types; (2) the technical input of bureaucrats who provide the data and the methodological expertise to produce a finished product; (3) the city council members who vote on a completed plan but who do not necessarily

171

participate in manipulating the plan's substance; and, (4) the community members who make recommendations resulting in only cosmetic changes. The above influence factors appear to occur in San Antonio especially if influence appears to lie more in the hands of the business community who seem to almost totally control the local state apparatus. The role of a minority mayor, like any other mayor of a local liberal democratic state, appears to be primarily responsible for cementing the relationship between the public and private sectors. Although they appear to be "strange bedfellows" minority mayors require the support of the business community to overcome the racial polarization of voters. On the other hand, the business community needs the minority mayor to mollify any criticism for developmental activities that may arise from the low income minority communities.

In attempting to answer the question of "who has more influence during the land use decisionmaking process?" one must consider the imperceptible power of history and ideology which directly affect the actions of those making decisions. The question then becomes which is more powerful, the political actor's thoughts or actions? If one assumes that one's thoughts must govern one's actions, then ideas carry the most influence during any decisional process. These ideas are molded and born in the decision maker's mind throughout their lifetime. In the United States this process is designed to imbue citizens with basic capitalist values and attitudes. Then the exercise of political power during the decisional process can be characterized differently as one considers different stages of the process and the roles played by the different actors involved at a particular stage of the process. Consequently, although history, represented by existing land uses, significantly affects any plan's substance, the collective participation by members of the business community in the decision making process insures the continuation of the basic economic status quo. This insures that the continued developmental and growth patterns of San Antonio will proceed in the same general direction in the future insuring the continued racial and social segregation of Anglos from Latinos and rich from the poor. So that the traditional method of

172

pursuing economic development appears to be at the root of the racial and social segregation endemic to San Antonio. While the changing face of the electoral process insures that racial minority group members must continuously struggle to gain control of the political apparatus. The two structures work in tandem insuring that Latinos will continually find themselves at or near the bottom of a liberal democratic society.

Chapter Five

A Dynamical Theory of the State

and

Latino Politics

There are two foci in this volume. The first is to explore some different thoughts concerning the theory of the state; the second is to place Latino politics within the "new" framework presented here generated by the "different" thoughts concerning the state. Although this work's intent was not to reconstruct or reinvent the theory of the state, a different way of thinking concerning the state has evolved leading to a broader theoretical framework within which future research endeavors can proceed. The discussion in this volume has also led to a deeper understanding of the place of Latinos within American political society.

This essay began with a review of liberal democratic thinking concerning the modern state. It is a general review because this volume is not intended as a complete or thorough critique of liberal democracy. What is intended is a review of the general principles of liberal democratic thought that underlie the modern state's structure. As a result the first assumption made in this essay is simply that *the state is a structure, a complex "matrix of influence," if you will, of interrelated institutions and processes bound together by an ideological value system bathed in liberal democratic principles.* A second assumption of this essay is that *the principle reason that the liberal democratic state has survived, at least the one in the United States of America, for over two hundred years is that the structural matrix is not a static construct but a dynamical one.* The political system or structure, then, is flexible and able to absorb, integrate, and socialize any, or most, forces that may threaten its integrity. Some of the systemic characteristics that make this matrix dynamic are the various types of institutions and processes, particularly the manner in which they are structured, which socialize or neutralize conflict within the system. Finally, the matrix is shrouded by the mystification mechanisms, such as the media, that continuously provide the general population with images and feelings that "although things are bad, they could be worse, and are far better than in other societies." In short, the mystification mechanisms also provide a propagandization/socialization machine for both the state and the private sectors (Herman and Chomsky, 1988).

Although, the institutional machinations are designed to maintain both a class structure and a system of unequal relationships between classes they do so in ways that make the general population feel that the opposite is true. The periodicity of elections allows the general population to think and feel that even though times appear socially or economically poor, another election will come where various political actors can be replaced. Or, even if politicians cannot be replaced, general social conditions will not remain uncomfortable for any great period of time and will improve eventually. Although many public policy decisions are ideologically decided, the explicit rationale for ruling against the interests of low-income and Latino communities are generally technical in nature. For instance, in voting rights or affirmative action cases courts will base their decisions on the lack of standing or the lack of jurisdiction or the fact that a district is "strange looking," and so forth. Or, in economic development decisions, lack of investing, buying power, availability of space, or an appropriate work force are used as excuses to inhibit developmental activities in low-income communities.

The second set of circumstances has been hailed as one of the strengths of liberal democratic societies. That is the expectations that elections will regularly

175

occur thereby allowing voters to "throw out the rascals" at the next available time if the people are dissatisfied with their performance. This expectation is what prevents revolutions from occurring in the "more developed or advanced" liberal democracies of the world because it serves as a structural mechanism that diffuses societal and political conflict. This is one of the structural features or characteristics that distinguishes liberal democracies from other forms of social-political systems. Finally, there is a constant proclamation by the media economic experts that economic downturns are inevitable because they are simply systemic and/or seasonal adjustments to an overly active market. Or, even more simplistically, the same experts deem the downturns statistical aberrations. Nevertheless, by conceiving of the state as a dynamical, as opposed to a static, construct one can both better trace the evolution of a state from the thoughts that gave birth to the state to what it has become over a two hundred year period of time and place the socialization process of the state within that evolutionary context. One may even be able to obtain a "peek" as to where the system is going to look like given the ability to identify certain major forces that may affect the state.

What, then, can one say concerning Latino politics given the assumption of a dynamical state? Another question, much more difficult to answer but more specific, follows from the first. Assuming that the state is a dynamical system, what does this say for Latino empowerment? What sorts of political strategies and tactics should Latinos pursue given the constant evolution of the liberal democratic state to reinforce itself against the intrusion of new players within its structure of power? Will Latinos eventually advance throughout liberal democracy's structures, both political and social, as other "new" groups have? Or, will they remain in a political "nether land" like the African Americans where only a few do well by American standards while the vast remainder of the group stays at the bottom of society's social structure? The answers to some of these questions raise other questions concerning the viability of voting, of participating within society, of continued protest, or of exiting from this society by opting for some sort of nationalistic political strategy? Finally, does the fact that liberal democratic society generates and maintains unequal social conditions make any difference? Is inequality wrong and, if it is, what should be done to alleviate it? If one concludes that inequality is not wrong? Why is this so? Cannot a long lasting social system, one as large and complex as that of the United States, exist as a liberal democracy without the existence of social inequality?

Although the two issues, the dynamical nature of the liberal democratic state and the state of Latino politics in the United States of America, appear as separate issues they are inextricably intertwined. Nevertheless, the first part of this concluding chapter is dedicated to a review of the comments on the dynamical theory of the state, while the second part of the chapter focuses on the relationship between the state and the Latino community.

The Dynamical State and Latinos

That the liberal democratic state is constantly changing form, from one historical era to another goes without saying. However, why the changes occur, under what circumstances these changes occur, and what the consequences and implications are of these changes appear as the most important questions that must be addressed. It was pointed out earlier that a liberal democratic state is composed of institutions and institutional arrangements that find their definition, both structurally and operationally, in liberal democratic principles. So that the scope and depth of the state's foci depend upon what a society will allow given the perceptions and actions of various individual political actors and/or groups. Essentially, this is played out as a power struggle over control of the public policy agenda. Sometimes this power struggle occurs in the electoral arena, sometimes it occurs in the media, and sometimes in the clash between mass movements such as the civil rights movement versus the intransigence of traditional political institutions. Nevertheless, political power is such, within a liberal democracy, that one person cannot dominate the entire structure. Political power is diffused throughout the structure and wielded, to different degrees, depending upon some combination of the individual attributes of the person, their place within society,

177

and the group or class to which they belong (Foucault, 1972). However, the composition of the political actors or regime tends to change throughout the historical life of the state due to a broad array of factors ranging from the interests of the group or class, whether the group or class has been able to retain its place within society, and so forth. What causes political power to change hands from individual to individual, group to group, class to class, and regime to regime is the changing situation of society itself (Marx, 1964).

This particular view of the distribution of power came about because of a continuing debate in the academy. Although much has been written on this topic most of the interesting debates occur at panels at the annual meetings of organizations such as The American Political Science Association or The American Sociological Association, over the adequacy of "traditional theories" such as pluralism, elite or systems theories, and structuralism. The debates appear to remain because their closure can never be achieved for a broad variety of reasons. Chief among these reasons is that the "traditional theories" have only been tested on a micro-level so that one can only obtain a picture of how one or the other of the theories functions in some cities or how the theory is applicable to the administration of certain state functions or programs. This makes it difficult to universalize about the theory and leaves the "door open" for additional debate or dialogue. Sometimes the debates remain because of the vested interests of some personalities not wanting to see "their theories" challenged and set aside by a "new or competing" idea. The proposers of the new theories will point out the shortcomings of the old theories while the defenders of the old theories will point out the immaturity of the new theories.

The literature on how racial minority groups "fit into the bigger political picture" is also mixed in that there does not appear to be any agreement over whether a racial succession model is a better explanatory model than the incorporation, regime, or internal colonial models. This volume is designed to take sides. It is a call to understand a political system as a dynamical matrix of institutional arrangements that change over time due to an unlimited array of factors that affect the matrix throughout its lifetime. Within this matrix Latinos find themselves victimized and subject to whatever public policy decisions evolve from the matrix. In short, Latinos are objectified to the matrix only able to react to any public policy decision that flows from the "web of influence" dominating the matrix. As a result, there appears to be a certain degree of accuracy in both "traditional racial oppression" models that dominate this sub-discipline of sociology—the racial succession and internal colonial models. According to the racial succession model Latinos will become successful in the United States once they can overcome the limitations placed upon them by their culture such as their language, personableness and culturally induced perceptions of how one's life will evolve (Moynihan, 1965 and Banfield, 1970). The inability to speak English will keep Latinos from obtaining an appropriate education that, in turn, will allow them to effectively and successfully participate in the market. The personable nature of Latinos will keep them from competing in all arenas of American life. And, their fatalism will "freeze" them into not trying to participate in society. Once these culturally induced barriers are overcome, Latinos will become full-fledged members of American society. So it is the fault of Latinos themselves that keeps them at the lower rungs of America's social structure.

The internal colonial model, which is a hybrid of colonial models made popular in the 1950s and 1960s, is interesting in itself and goes far in explaining why Latinos and other "out groups" have failed to become as integrated into American society as some would wish. The model was elaborated initially by Robert Blauner (1972) in describing the plight of the African American community, was extended to describe the oppressed social, economic and political conditions of Chicanos by Mario Barrera, Carlos Muñoz, and Charles Ornelas (1972). According to the internal colonial model, forces, groups and individuals, "external" to the community control the social and economic conditions of Chicanos. Domination of Chicanos is motivated principally by a type of racism that is a subset of traditional White European racial ideologies. These ideologies generally excuse the domination because the dominated groups are perceived as

179

being intellectually and culturally inferior and this inferiority may be due to their economically underdeveloped situation or their genetic inferiority. Although some would argue that these perceptions have passed from the scene one only needs to look at the recent work of Herrnstein and Murray (1994) as evidence to the contrary. Nevertheless, a principle characteristic of the internally colonized was that "the dominant and subordinate populations are intermingled, so that there is no geographically distinct 'metropolis' separate from the 'colony' (González Casanova, 1965)." (Cited in Barrera, 1979) Both Blauner (1972) and Barrera pointed out that the significant problem, Blauner labeled it a "major defect" in his study, was that the model" lacks a conception of American society as a total structure." Barrera offered a synthesis of the internal colonial and class segmentation model as a means to address the deficiency of the internal colonial model (1979). Barrera's "new and improved model" describes Chicanos as existing as segments within all class levels of American society yet they find themselves subject to the effects of discrimination within these classes. So, although there may be Chicano capitalists or Chicanos populating the ranks of the middle class they still will find their economic well being more susceptible to market fluctuations than others of the same social classes. Those Chicanos belonging to the working and poor classes will find themselves performing work deemed appropriate to their race (Mexican work) or subject to the discriminatory effects of a dual-wage system where they are paid less than Anglos for the same work performed. Regardless, in Barrera's model one finds vastly more Chicanos populating the lower class rungs of society than populating the ranks of the wealthy.

Most importantly, Barrera and Blauner, shifted the blame for the social and economic exclusion and domination of African Americans and Chicanos from the people themselves to the dominating effects engendered by the greater society. The racial succession models, based on the immigration experiences of the Irish, Italians and Jews placed the blame on the "cultural deprivation" of Latinos—their culture was less than appropriate to allow success in liberal democratic society.

Barrera and Blauner turned the blame back on the system itself. Emphatically stating that the nature and normal machinations of capitalism itself is the principal cause for Latinos remaining at the bottom of American society.

Significantly absent from the discussion of America's social structure, whether, one champions the racial succession or internal colonial/class segmentation models or any of their varieties, is any attempt to link the social to the political systems. In short, there is an absence of any attempt to link society and the state together. Barrera does appear to prefer the analysis proffered by Nicos Poulantzas but only does so in passing (1979). Barrera's social model, I feel, is accurate and the reasons Chicanos specifically and Latinos generally find themselves where they are in America's social structure is due to the fact that the matrix of influence's design, offered here, and normal functioning is guided by an ideological system that mitigates against the ability of one person or one group of individuals to change the matrix's orientation. Essentially, the complex nature and, sometimes, size of the matrix allows for so many political power access points that it is almost impossible to control them all. Chaos or, more appropriately, non-linear dynamics theory also points out the futility of attempting to identify all possible variables that may affect the matrix or the exact moment or intensity with which the variables will affect the matrix.

The case studies in Chapter Four which speak to the structural biasedness underlying land use decisions and electoral politics in San Antonio were designed to proffer a "hint" at both the structural and dynamical nature of the state's power. On one level political power is exercised by a broad array of actors including politicians, bureaucrats, and some community leaders. However, two non-human entities appear to wield as much or more political power than all the political actors combined, the existence of past decisions as exemplified by large physical structures that dominate the landscape of a city limiting the available developmental space and options and the permeation of ideology throughout the decisional process. So that political power becomes not just the actions of individuals manipulating the institutions and laws of the state but it becomes something almost both undetectable, permanent and oftentimes overlooked. Ideological values find their way into policy decisions because they represent the dominant values of a society that have been transmitted to decision makers throughout their lifetimes. This transmission has occurred through the normal socialization processes almost all persons undergo as they grow and mature naturally (Therborn, 1982). The combination of representatives of particular social classes controlling positions of power, both in the public and in the private sectors coupled with the physical features, both artificial and natural, of a large city that limit the number and types of developmental choices held together by a two-century old ideological perception of the relationship between the state and the private sector creates a structure that makes it almost impossible for Latinos or persons from lower social classes from exercising any significant political influence. This includes being able to exercise at least enough political influence to affect the public policy agenda in any substantive manner. Unless, of course an issue pertinent to the out group is championed by some institutionalized power broker or group. This "political absorption" process is another mechanism the state utilizes to socialize conflict. The inclusion of the new issue, on the other hand, tends to change the state's structure as well. Examples of this proliferate throughout the history of the labor movement in the United States where issues important to workers, championed by unions, then political parties gave birth to laws, regulations, and bureaucracies governing the relations between workers and management. In the initial stage of this struggle one finds the issues championed only by communists and other agitators by the time the struggle is over one finds the creation of the Department of Labor and the Office of Occupational Safety and Health Administration (OSHA).

The complex nature of the state's matrix, which on the surface appears as fragmentation, where power seems to be defused among levels and between institutional branches, is what makes it difficult to gain control of the entire structure. On one hand this complexity mitigates against the ability of any one group, class, or individual from gaining control of the entire structure. What allows the public policy processes of the state to be dominated by the interests of capital is the same fragmented nature and the profusion of the ideological perception legitimizing the role of the public/private nexus throughout the state. The ability of private interests to influence the electoral structure, fund think tanks and experts, provide research and information to public decision makers, influence the media and public opinion, and control the resources that allow them to be the principle beneficiaries of most public policy decisions is what allows them to exercise influence at a broad array of decisional nodes throughout the state (Domhoff, 1990; Dye, 1976a, 1984b, 1992c).

The exercise of private power within and over the state apparatus is, simultaneously, mythologized and mystified by the predominant democratic ideology that constantly sets the "people" above the state. Throughout the socialization process American society is bombarded with the myth of popular sovereignty, which Roelofs (1992) traces to liberal democratic thought beginning with Hobbes and culminating with Jefferson. This "democratic mythology" masks the reality of how political influence is exercised on a day-to-day basis by the players themselves. Political players who are driven by self-interests and the exigencies of time to accomplish and achieve certain goals and tasks; by the media who are constantly motivated by survival interests; by the educational system that perpetuates the myth through narrowly focused curricula and teachers; and, by the infusion of liberal democratic principles and ideals in administrative, judicial, and professional interpretations of social and political problems and their solutions. The mystification and mythologization of reality, then, can be both deliberate and unintentional. Some persons may wish to hide their influence in order to not create a legitimation crisis (Wolfe, 1977; Habermas 1975) that would shatter the myth in the eyes of the people and result in the inability to effectively wield political power. Other groups or classes simply do not care or think of the consequences of what they are doing and pursue their self-interests on a daily basis not cognizant that they may be acting in an undemocratic manner or creating externalities harmful to various sectors of society.

183

Claus Offe's model, presented in Chapter Two which states that the state is a collection of filtering systems that eliminate public policy decisions that are not favorable to the interests of capital as a whole, appears to appropriately describe the matrix and the internal institutional relationships of the state matrix. That the land use decisions underlying economic development in San Antonio favor the general interests of the private sector is apparent if one assumes, as does Offe, that any developmental decisions produce results that maintain the general social conditions of the city's social structure, enhance the property values in the neighborhoods populated by the city's higher income and non-minority communities, and provide opportunities that only a small group of investors or developers can pursue. The decisions by the developers serve to create and enhance wealth while at the same time produce and exacerbate social segregation and inequality. In Offe's perception these decisions and consequences do not have to be made deliberately but may also be consequences of a society's "normal way of thinking." Essentially, social inequality becomes an unintended, natural consequence of capitalist developmental decisions.

The proof for the assertion that the state filtering system favors the interests of the private sector or capital over those of Latinos and other low-income communities in San Antonio possesses three facets. The first is the extent to which there has been a lack of improvement in the income levels of Latinos in the city. Additionally, the value of property in the Latino community of San Antonio has remained relative unchanged in relationship to that of the Anglo, high-income communities. Finally, that there has not been any social movement away from the predominantly Latino communities of 1970 to what they are in 2001.

The data in Chapter Four point out that the median incomes of the Latino communities in San Antonio, although increasing over a twenty five year period, did not increase at the same rate as the median incomes for Anglos. This discrepancy, however, may also be attributed to a number of other factors such as variable educational levels, the existence of differing types of income generating opportunities in both communities, a lack of mobility on the part of Latinos, and so forth. Each of the factors can be found to be fundamentally dependent upon the type of economic development decisions made in San Antonio. The quality of educational opportunities for Latinos is heavily dependent upon the value of real property in their neighborhoods, which in San Antonio is far lower than that of the predominantly Anglo neighborhoods. This differential in educational opportunity between Anglos and Latinos translates into differing levels of income levels later in life (Kozol, 1972). Most importantly, a good quality education also translates into a better informed citizenry that can play a more active and knowledgeable role in the political and public life of a society (Denvir, 2001). So that one can clearly see a linear relationship between the types and locations of economic development decisions and the median income levels of both Anglos and Latinos. A lack or minimal amount of economic development activity in a community results in lower property values which, in turn, results in a community's inability to generate a significant amount of money to provide a good quality education for its children. On the other hand, the opposite is also true. Where economic development decisions favor the interests of investors as represented by the location, type, and scope of development activity in already property wealthy areas, one will discover higher property values, generating higher property tax revenues, resulting in more money being available for the provision of public schools. The end result is the maintenance of two socially segregated communities that appear to become more and more segregated as the years go by. But the communities are not simply being maintained in a segregated condition the segregation appears to intensify the longer the state's decisional structure continues to be dominated by the public/private nexus which places the interests of the private sector above those of low-income and Latino communities.

The other segment of the proof compliments the first in that the data in Chapter Four indicate that not only is San Antonio's Latino community falling further behind the Anglo community, as far as income is concerned, but the percentage of Latinos living within the traditional Mexican enclaves appears to be

185

increasing. Essentially, traditional Latino enclaves are becoming more dense, more Latino, if you will. For example, in San Antonio, Texas the heavily Latino population residing in the southern tier of the city has increased from 60% of the population in 1970 to 80% of the population by 1994. Further typifying the situation, the most Latino school district, the one that has been the plaintiff in some of the most important educational financing litigation before both the United States and Texas Supreme courts, the Edgewood Independent School District, has gone from 90% Latino in 1967 to 96% in 1994. Although Latinos have been moving into what traditionally have been viewed as Anglo enclaves of San Antonio there appears to be an increase in density of Latinos in traditional Latino enclaves as well. Essentially, the increased percentage of Latinos in already heavily populated Latino communities simply indicates that racial segregation is keeping pace with the economic segregation that continues in the city. The economic development that has occurred in San Antonio, then, appears not to be benefiting the low-income or Latino communities generally. In short, whatever benefits Latinos have derived from the normal manner in which the local state plans for economic development are not apparent. In fact, one can conclude that the normal decisional processes of the liberal democratic local state appear to reinforce the social inequalities already existing within the city.

Latino Politics

Why the Latino community appears to be excluded from the decisional structure can be explained partially by the nature of how the various political actors are chosen or self-selected to participate in politics locally. The case of Henry Cisneros in San Antonio provides some evidence in this respect.

Cisneros' election marked the first time since 1842 that a Latino had been elected to the mayoralty. Mr. Cisneros' election marked the "political incorporation" of Mexican Americans into the policy formation process of the city. Although the mayor's office is statutorily weak, Mr. Cisneros found himself in a position to influence the public policy agenda simply through his magnetic personality and personal charm. Additionally, in spite of the fact that San Antonio does not have the national standing of a city such as Los Angeles it has historically been an important link with Mexico socially and economically. The social history of San Antonio has been littered with racism and racist activities from the forced exile of Mexicans after the 1836 war to the use of "Mexican Rooms" in the public school system as late as the 1960s to racial intimidation tactics during elections in the 1980s. Cisneros' election was supposed to mark the political arrival of Latinos in both San Antonio and national politics. After eight years of Cisneros' tenure, however, the Latino community still found themselves geographically and socially isolated and segregated. On a theoretical level this can be answered partially by the biased nature of the filtering process operant throughout the liberal democratic state discussed in Chapter 2. On a more substantive level, however, this filtering process operates only through the actions of the political actors who populate the decisional structure from the policy formation through the implementation stages.

Cisneros was elected only with the active support of a significant part of the business community. This was due principally to the power struggle that was raging within the business community of San Antonio during the early part of the 1970s. Nevertheless, the segment of the business community that supported Cisneros found that his pro-growth developmental philosophy mirrored theirs and saw his candidacy as an important key to "gaining the upper hand" in the war with the "old line" business community. The economic development policies instituted by Cisneros once he became mayor were simply designed to smooth the way through the city's bureaucratic maze, to attract new business to the city, and encourage development through tax incentives. None of these policies were designed to improve the quality of life of the city's low-income or Latino communities. This was accomplished principally through the simple passage of a few city ordinances and the modification of a few already existing city offices. This combined with the development community's takeover of the city's planning commission guaranteed that any developmental policies that emanated from San Antonio City Government after 1980 would be written to favor the interests of

187

developers. So that in San Antonio, Texas the public/private nexus simply created a business environment where there is an almost complete absence of the public domain and all developmental decisions remain in the hands of the private sector.

The developer dominated city developmental process has resulted in bitter battles, both electoraly and legally, between the private sector and various community organizations over environmental issues particularly water and quality of life issues. These struggles appear to be the result of a continuing neglect, on the part of the private sector; to understand the community's needs in relationship to their developmental efforts. Fundamentally, the water struggle is caused by the developer's unlimited growth philosophy that dominates developmental activity not meshing with the fact that San Antonio possesses a water supply of unknown dimensions. This is compounded by the perception of the developers wishing to pursue development in the northern parts of the county that overlay the ecologically sensitive acquifer that holds the city's drinking water supply. This is further compounded by the fact that living within the acquifer are several species of animal, fish and plant life that are protected under the Federal Endangered Species Act[1]. As the data in Chapter Four indicate it appears that both environmentalists and Latinos are not winning the development struggles because activity seems to have increased to the north where the acquifer recharge zone lies. All of this recent developmental activity coincided with Henry Cisneros' first mayoral victory. The quality of life issues revolve around the refusal of city officials to negotiate "living wage" contracts with businesses relocating to San Antonio and the city's propensity to grant "property tax abatements" as incentives to businesses wishing to relocate to the city. The former policy is designed to encourage the relocation of businesses that pay wages above the accepted minimum wage. The latter policy tends to shift the property tax burden to homeowners and also deprives local school districts of much needed revenues.

---

[1] This debate is being waged currently, again. The Professional Golfers Association wishes to construct a professional golfing "recreation complex" replete with three golf courses, hotels, single family dwellings, and shopping malls immediately on top of the aquifer's recharge zone. The city council and the mayor, Mr. Ed Garza, find themselves caught between the development

It appears then, that the incorporation of racial minority group politicians into the political process in San Antonio has brought "mixed blessings." This conclusion agrees with those of Browning, Marshall, and Tabb (1990). At the same time the election of Henry Cisneros did little substantively for the city's Latino community. The data in Chapter Four appear to indicate that, economically and socially, very little has changed for Latinos in San Antonio during the last 20 to 25 years. On the other hand the election of a Latino mayor has brought much needed public notice to this minority community at all political levels.

The relative weakness of the mayor's office notwithstanding, two important aspects of San Antonio's political environment continuously will prevent Latinos from gaining substantive control over the city's political structure in the near future. The more important of the two aspects is the racial tension that underlies social relations in the city and that are reflected in the racially polarized city council elections. This, in itself, will prohibit the election of another Latino to the mayor's office for the foreseeable future, unless of course an attractive Latino candidate who sees "eye-to-eye" with the development community and who, as a result, wins its support comes forth. These conditions were met when Mr. Ed Garza, a landscape architect with a local development firm, was elected mayor in 2001. Mr. Garza's candidacy was helped significantly by the lack of a strong Anglo opponent allowing Mr. Garza to defeat a field of ten candidates garnering 58.6% of the votes cast in the primary that also allowed him to avoid a runoff. Lacking the "special circumstances," the presence of a viable opponent and gathering the overwhelming support of the business community, the only Latino representation one will see in San Antonio's future will come from Hispanic politicians elected from the majority Latino city council districts.

The second aspect of San Antonio's political landscape that will act as a barrier to the substantive empowerment of Latinos is the dynamic nature of the local electoral process. This is exemplified through the constant changing of the

community and environmentalists. The outcome of this struggle will determine the political and economic balance in San Antonio for the foreseeable future.

electoral "rules of the game" making it continuously difficult for Latinos to win and hold office in San Antonio. This was the case when, after the courts forced the city to change from at-large elections to single member districts to alleviate the under-representation of the Latino community, a movement began to limit the terms in office. As the truth concerning the antidemocratic nature of term limits surfaced another movement began to "consolidate the city and county governments." Finally, the Republican Texas State Attorney General (a Latino no less) felt that given the improved state of race relations in Texas the state government should petition the national government to have Texas removed from coverage under the Federal Voting Rights Act. In short, the electoral rules and structures of the local state appear to change continuously making the acquisition of political power by Latinos an equally continuously changing challenge. It seems that just when Latinos have developed a comfortable understanding of the electoral process the structure's integrity changes. The effect on Latinos and other out-groups is that they must constantly relearn the rules and develop new strategies to achieve electoral empowerment. What this means as far as being able to exercise any degree of influence over the public policy process is that there is a lack of consistency in Latino representation. This results in an inability to consistently set forth a coherent public policy agenda on a regular basis. This lack of consistent and stable Latino representation may also have resulted in lower turnout rates and lower numbers of Latinos running for city council office in San Antonio. My suspicion is based in the notion that the rapid "turn over" of elected local officials tends to flood the political market place with so many unknown and inexperienced politicians that the electoral map becomes confusing to the Latino electorate. Additionally, as was mentioned in Chapter Four, term limits tends to create a "revolving door" effect, turning out city council members so often that voters may be allowing the tem limitation law to remove elected officials and may not see the need to vote.

An interesting paradox associated with the dynamical nature of the matrix is that the local state presents Latinos and other political "out-groups" with opportunities to win elections, influence policy, or both. The moment that the state is challenged and forced to change, such as before, during, and shortly after the switch between at-large and single member district elections, is the precise moment that the system is the weakest and most vulnerable. These are the appropriate moments for the mobilization and coalition building efforts that can change the political and public policy landscapes of not simply San Antonio's local state but any liberal democratic state.

A question still remains if the state is changing form why does the general social structure of society remain relatively unchanged? This question is based upon the discussion presented in Chapter Three where the dynamic nature of the state structure was presented. Evidence was presented to show that the local state, dominating San Antonio, Texas, changed form from one historical period to another. Yet, the social data presented in Chapter Four indicated that the Latino community's social situation remained relatively unchanged during a particularly high growth period even while enjoying electoral successes. This is not a paradox that cannot be unraveled; rather this speaks to both the dynamic nature and relative autonomy of the state.

The state's dynamic nature allows it to change during a normal evolutionary cycle as depicted in Chapter Three. Various political situations, changing public and private perceptions and expectations, changing demographics, and the changing structure of the economy all affected not only the bureaucratic structure of the state but also the electoral process and the sort of individuals who populated the city government. Like any liberal democratic state, however, it is not primary in society; the state is a concoction of human beings who design the structure to suit their intentions. Additionally, both their intentions and the extent to which they can restructure the state is dependent upon the social structure.

The local state in San Antonio is modeled upon the same liberal democratic principles that gave birth to the national state over two hundred years ago. The intention was not to alleviate poverty or eradicate social inequality but

191

to provide a stable social setting or structure in order that the private business sector could and can peacefully pursue its goals. The state was to intervene only in time of crisis such as during full-scale warfare or to prevent extensive social unrest among the population. At the national level this was evident during major wars or economic depressions when required total mobilization of national resources was required. At the local level, the state only mobilizes its full police powers to insure that the local population goes about its daily business without doing too much harm to each other. So the local state has been characterized as both the protector of private property and individual liberties as well as an agent of social control. Although the state will change due to various social forces this does not mean that the general social structure will also change. It appears, however, that the opposite may be true. In other words, if the social structure changes dramatically, for instance if Latinos were to suddenly become the dominant racial or ethnic group in American society and capitalism were to take a radical turn in the way it is managed, controlled, and what it produces, then the state will also change. That is assuming that Latinos were to have an agenda not compatible with the basic principles of capitalism and liberal democracy, which is a relatively spurious argument, given the current research on the belief structures of Latinos (delaGarza, et al, 1992). The state would have to change in order to accommodate the severe social restructuring that would occur or the state would collapse. Essentially, as long as the social means of production remain the same the state will change only marginally, however, when the social change is dramatic the state must also change dramatically. When the state changes only marginally, the social structure remains relatively unchanged. If, however, the state were to change dramatically through "imperial overreach" (Kennedy, 1987), defeat in warfare, or severe economic depression then there **may** be extreme shifts in a society's social structure.

What limits the state's scope and depth of intrusion in the social world are the complete set of liberal democratic ideological principles that are used in the interpretation of social problems by bureaucrats, politicians, and judges who

192

oversee the functioning of the state. The economic interpretations of investors, government planners, and judges which define social conditions a certain way, solutions for those problems, and ways in which to implement the solutions for the problems insure that the state retains and maintains its autonomy and distance from the social world. What has been interpreted by some (Domhoff, 1990) as the autonomy of the state is really an ideologically enforced distance. This was evident in the manner economic development is planned in San Antonio. If the state were to define itself as the true champion of the poor and socially oppressed it would do so through the manner in which it makes legal and administrative decisions affecting the poor. However, the state in a liberal democracy is a state dominated and its structure and function is determined by the ideological orientation of how society is structured. A liberal democratic society is, by definition, a society that produces social inequality (Barrera, 1979). The function of a liberal democratic state is not to seek solutions for solving that inequality but to manage the inequality in such a manner as to make it palatable to all.

As far as Latinos in the United States generally and San Antonio specifically this means that they should not look to the state as an agent that will do something to alleviate their socially unequal conditions. Rather in that Latinos must look at the state as the enforcer of the colonization processes and the legitimizer of domination.

Bibliography

Altshuler, Alan. 1965. The City Planning Process: A Political Analysis. Ithaca, NY: Cornell University Press.

Bachrach, Peter and Morton Baratz. 1962. "The Two Faces of Power." American Political Science Review.

Baldassare, Mark. Editor. 1994. The Los Angeles Riots: Lessons For the Urban Future. San Francisco: Westview Press.

Banfield, Edward and James Q. Wilson. 1966. City Politics. NY: Vantage.

Banfield, Edward. 1970. The Unheavenly City. Boston: Little, Brown.

Barrera, Mario. 1979. Race and Class in the Southwest: A Theory of Racial Inequality. Notre Dame: University of Notre Dame Press.

Barrera, Mario, Carlos Muñoz, and Charles Ornelas. 1972. "The Barrio as an Internal Colony." In Harlan Hahn, ed. People and Politics in Urban Society. Los Angeles: Sage Publications.

Beard, Charles A. (1913) 1959. An Economic Interpretation of the Constitution of the United States. New York: The Macmillan Company.

Beard, Charles A. and Mary A. 1930. The Rise of American Civilization. NewYork: The Macmillan Company.

Bendix, John, Timothy Mitchell, Bertell Ollman, and Bartholomew Sparrow 1992. "Going Beyond the State?" American Political Science Review.

Bentham, Jeremy. (1776). A Fragment of Government. Edited with an introduction by F. C. Montague. 1980. Westport CN: Greenwood Press, Publishers.

Bickel, Alexander M. 1971. Reform and Continuity: The Electoral College, the Convention, and the Party System. NY: Harper & Row, Publishers.

Blauner, Robert. 1972. Racial Oppression in America. New York: Harper and Row.

Booth, J. A., Johnson, D. R., and Harris, R. J. 1983. The Politics of San Antonio Community, Progress and Power. Lincoln, NB: The University of Nebraska Press.

Boorstin, D.J. 1985. The Discoverers. New York: Random House.

Bridges, Amy. 1984. A City in the Republic: Antebellum New York and the Origins of MachinePolitics. NY: Cambridge University Press.

_____. 1998. Morning Glories: Municipal Reform in the Southwest. Princeton: Princeton University Press.

Bullard, Robert D., J. Eugene Grigsby III, & Charles Lee. Editors. 1994. Residential Apartheid:The American Legacy. Los Angeles: The University of California at Los Angeles.

Burchall, Graham, Colin Gordon, and Peter Miller, editors. 1991. The Foucault Effect: Studies inGovernmentality with Two Lectures by and an Interview with Michel Foucault. Chicago: The University of Chicago Press.

Carnoy, Martin. 1984. The State and Political Theory. Princeton, NJ: Princeton University Press.

Casey, Rick. 1985. "The End of the Developer War." San Antonio Monthly.

Dahl, R. 1961. Who Governs? New Haven: Yale University Press.

Davidson, Chandler. 1990. Race and Class in Texas Politics. Princeton, NJ: The Princeton University Press.

Davidson, Chandler and Bernard Grofman, editors. 1994. Quiet Revolution in the South: The Impact of the Voting Rights Act, 1965-1990. Princeton, NJ: Princeton University Press.

Davis, Mike. 1992. City of Quartz: Excavating the Future of Los Angeles. NY: Vintage Books.

De la Garza, et al. 1992. Latino Voices: Mexican, Puerto Rican, & Cuban Perspectives on American Politics. Boulder, CO: Westview Press.

195

Denvir, John. 2001. <u>Democracy's Constitution: Claiming the Privileges of American Citizenship.</u> Chicago: University of Illinois Press.

DeSipio, Louis. 1996. <u>Counting on the Latino Votes: Latinos as a New Electorate.</u> Charlottesville, VA: University of Virginia Press.

de Tocqueville, Alexis. 1945. <u>Democracy in America, Vol I.</u> New York: Vintage Books.

Diehl, Kemper and Jan Jarboe. 1985. <u>Cisneros: Portrait of an American.</u> San Antonio, TX: Corona Publishing Company.

Dolbeare, Kenneth and Edelman, Murray. 1981. <u>American Politics: Policies Power, and Change.</u> Lexington, MA: D.C. Heath and Company.

Domhoff, G. William. 1990. <u>The Power Elite and the State: How Policy is Made in America.</u> NY: Aldine De Gruyter.

Earle, Edward Mead, ed. 1937. <u>The Federalist: A Commentary on the Constitution of the United States.</u> New York: The Modern Library.

Easton, David. 1965. <u>A Systems Analysis of Political Life.</u> New York: John Wiley.

Engels, Frederick. 1891. "A Critique of the Draft Social-Democratic Programme of 1891" in <u>Marx-Engels. 1970. Selected Works. Vol. 3</u> Moscow.

_____. 1875. "Letter From Engels to Bebel." <u>Marx-Engels. 1970. Selected Works.</u> Moscow.

_____. 1978. <u>The Origin of the Family, Private Property and</u> theState. New York: International Publishers.

Engels, Frederick and Karl Marx. 1975. <u>The Holy Family, or Critique of Critical Criticism.</u> Moscow: Progress Publishers.

Easton, D. 1990. <u>The Analysis of Political Structure.</u> New York: Routledge Chapman and Hall, Inc.

Easton, David and Jack Dennis. 1969. <u>Children in the Political System: Origins of Political Legitimacy.</u> NY: McGraw-Hill Book Company.

Elkin, Stephen L. 1987. <u>City and Regime in the American Republic.</u> Chicago: The University of Chicago Press.

Farrand, Max, editor. 1911-32. The Records of the Federal Constitution of 1787. New Haven, CN: Yale University Press.

Flores, H. 1989. "The Selectivity of the Capitalist State." The Western Political Quarterly.

———. 1991. "Deconstruction and Chicano Politics: Coalition Building During the Cisneros Era." In R. E. Villarreal and N. G. Hernandez, Latinos and Political Coalitions: Political Empowerment for the 1990s. New York: Greenwood Press.

Giroux, Henry A. 1988. Schooling and the Struggle for Public Life: Critical Pedagogy in the Modern Age. Minneapolis, MN: University of Minnesota Press.

——— and David Purpel. 1983. The Hidden Curriculum and Moral Education. Berkeley, CA: McCutchan Publishing.

Gleick, J. 1987. Chaos: Making A New Science. New York: Penguin Books.

Goldberg, David Theo. 1997. Racial Subjects: Writing on Race in America. New York: Routledge.

Gomez-Quinones, Juan. 1990. Chicano Politics: Reality and Promise, 1940-1990. Albuquerque, NM: The University of New Mexico Press.

Gottlieb, Robert and Irene Wolt. 1977. Thinking Big. New York: G. P. Putnam's Sons.

Greenberg, E. S. and Mayer, T. F. 1990. Changes in the State: Causes and Consequences. Newbury Park, CA.: Sage Publications, Inc.

Habermas, Jurgen. 1977. Legitimation Crisis. Boston: Beacon Press.

Harvey, David. 1973. Social Justice and the City. Baltimore, MD: The Johns Hopkins University Press.
——————. 1989. The Condition of Postmodernity: An Enquiry into the Origins of Cultural Change. NY: Basil Blackwell.

Hayles, N. K. 1990. Chaos Bound: Orderly Disorder in Contemporary Literature and Science. New York: Cornell University Press.

——— 1991. Chaos and Order: Complex Dynamics in Literature and Science. Chicago: The University of Chicago Press.

Herman, Edward S. & Noam Chomsky. 1988. Manufacturing Consent:
The Political Economy of The Mass Media. New York: Pantheon Books.

Hernnstein, Richard J. and Charles Murray. 1994. The Bell Curve:
Intelligence and ClassStructure in American Life. New York: Basic
Books.

Hume, L. J. 1981. Bentham and Bureaucracy. Cambridge:
Cambridge University Press.

Jennings, M. Kent and Richard G. Niemi. 1974. The Political Character of
Adolescence: The Influence of Families and Schools. Princeton, NJ:
Princeton University Press.

Kellert, S. H. 1993. In the Wake of Chaos: Unpredictable Order in Dynamical
Systems. Chicago: The University of Chicago Press.

Kennedy, Paul. 1987. The Rise and Fall of Great Powers: Economic Change
and Military Conflict From 1500 to 2000. New York: Random House.

Kirby v Edgewood. S.W. 2d (1987).

Kozol, Jonathan. 1992. Savage Inequalities: Children in America's Schools.
New York:
Harper Collins.

Kramnick, Isaac. 1990. Republicanism and Bourgeois Radicalism: Political
Ideology in Late Eighteenth-Century England and America. Ithaca:
Cornell University Press.

Lamare, James W. 1997. Texas Politics: Economics, Power, and Policy. 6th Ed.
Belmont, CA:
West Publishing Co.

Langton, Kenneth P. and M. Kent Jennings. 1968. "Political Socialization and
the High School Civis Curriculum in the United States." American
Political Science Review.

Lau v Nichols, 414 U.S. 563 (1974).

Lindblom, Charles E. 1977. Politics and Markets: The World's Political
_____ Economic Systems. New York: Basic Books.

Lorenz, Edward N. 1993. The Essence of Chaos. Seattle: The University of Washington Press.

Lowi, Theodore J. 1979. The End of Liberalism: The Second Republic of the United States. New York: W. W. Norton and Company.

Lustig, R. Jeffrey. 1982. Corporate Liberalism: The Origins of Modern American Political Theory, 1890-1920. Berkeley, CA: University of California Press.

Lyotard, J. 1984. The Postmodern Condition: A Report on Knowledge. Minneapolis, MN: The University of Minnesota Press.

Macpherson, C.B. 1977. The Life and Times of Liberal Democracy. London: Oxford University Press.

Marbury v Madison, 1 Cr. 137 (1803).

Marx, Karl. (1857-58). 1952. Pre-Capitalist Economic Formations. New York: International Publishers.

_____. 1963. The Eighteenth Brumaire of Louis Bonaparte. New York: International Publishers.

Mayer, David. 1987. The Constitutional Thought of Thomas Jefferson. Charlotsville, VA: University Press of Virginia.

Miliband, Ralph. 1969. The State in Capitalist Society. London: Weidenfeld and Nicolson.

Mill, James. 1820. An Essay on Government. With an Introduction by Sir Ernest Barker 1937. Cambridge University Press.

Montague, F.C., ed. 1980. A Fragment on Government by Jeremy Bentham. New York: Greenwood Press.

Montejano, D. 1987. Anglos and Mexicans in the Making of Texas, 1836-1986. Austin, TX: The University of Texas Press.

National Association of Latino Elected and Appointed Officials. 1993. 1993, National Roster of Hispanic Elected Officials. Los Angeles, CA: NALEO Educational Fund, Inc.

O'Connor, James. 1987. The Meaning of Crisis: A Theoretical Introduction. NY: Basil Blackwell.

Parenti, Michael. 1994. Land of Idols: Political Mythology in America. NY: St. Martin's Press.

Peirce, Neal R. 1968. The People's President: The Electoral College in American History and the Direct Vote Alternative. NY: Simon & Schuster.

Peters, William. 1987. A More Perfect Union. NY: Crown Publishers, Inc.

Poulantzas, Nicos. 1978. State, Power, Socialism. London: New Left Books.

Prigogine, I. and Stengers, I. 1984. Order Out of Chaos: Man's New Dialogue With Nature. New York: Bantam Books.

Reagan, Michael. 1963. The Managed Economy. New York: Oxford University Press.

Rice Center. 1985. Research Profile 2. San Antonio, Texas.

Rifkin, Jeremy. 1980. Entropy. NY: Bantam Books.

Riordan, William, J. 1994. Plunkitt of Tammany Hall. NY: Bedford.

Rosenblum, Nancy L. 1978. Bentham's Theory of the Modern State. Cambridge, MA: Harvard University Press.

Rossiter, Clinton. 1963. The Political Thought of the American Revolution: Part Three of Seedtime of the Republic. New York: Harcourt, Brace and World, Inc.

Russell, Bertrand. 1945. A History of Western Philosophy. New York: Simon and Schuster.

Rutland, Robert, et al, eds. 1977. The Papers of James Madison. Chicago: The University of Chicago Press.

San Antonio Independent School District v Rodriguez, 411 U.S. 1 (1973).

Sanders, Luther Lee. 1976 "How to Win Elections in San Antonio the Good Government Way,
1955 – 1971." M.A. Thesis, St. Mary's University, 1975.

Schroyer, Trent. 1973. The Critique of Domination: The Origins and Development of Critical Theory. NY: George Braziller.

Schwartz, Bernard. 1993. A History of the Supreme Court. New York: Oxford University Press.

Sibley, Mulford Q. 1970. Political Ideas and Ideologies: A History of Political Thought. New York: Harper and Row, Publishers.

Smith, Adam. [1776] 1937. An Inquiry Into the Nature and Causes of the Wealth of Nations. New York: The Modern Library.

_____. [1759] 1976. The Theory of Moral Sentiments. Indianapolis: Liberty Classics.

Stewart, Joseph and Kenneth Meier. 1991. The Politics of Hispanic Education. Stoneybrook, NY: State University of New York.

Stewart, William S. 1988. Understanding Politics: The Cultures of Societies and the Structures of Government. Novato, CA: Chandler and Sharp Publishers, Inc.

Stone, C.N. 1989. Regime Politics: Governing Atlanta, 1946-1988. Lawrence, KS: The University of Kansas Press.

Swanstrom, Todd. 1985. The Crisis of Growth Politics: Cleveland, Kucinch, and the Challenge of Urban Populism. Philadelphia: Temple University Press.

Tapper, Ted. 1976. Political Education and Stability: Elite Responses to Political Conflict. NY: John Wiley & Sons.

Teixeira, Roy A. 1992. The Disappearing American Voter. Washington, D.C. The Brookings Institution.

Therborn, Goran. 1982. The Ideology of Power and the Power of Ideology. London: Verso Editions and New Left Books.

Turner, Bryan S. Editor. 1990. Theories of Modernity and Postmodernity. London: Sage Publications Ltd.

Vaughan, C.E. 1971. The Political Writings of Jean Jacques Rousseau. Two Volumes. New York: Burt Franklin.

Vincent, Andrew. 1987. Theories of the State. New York: Basil Blackwell Inc.

Warner, Sam B. 1968. The Private City: Philadelphia in Three Periods of Growth. Philadelphia, PA: University of Pennsylvania Press.

Weissberg, Robert. 1974. Political Learning, Political Choice, and Democratic Citizenship. Englewood Cliffs, NJ: Prentice-Hall, Inc.

West, Cornel. 1993. Race Matters. Boston: Beacon Press.

White v Regester, 412 U.S. 55 (1973).

Wolfe, Alan. 1977. The Limits of Legitimacy. New York: The Free Press.

Wolfinger, Raymond E. and Steven J. Rosenstone. 1980. Who Votes? New Haven: Yale University Press.

Wolin, Sheldon S. 1960. Politics and Vision: Continuity and Innovation in Western Political Thought. Boston: Little, Brown and Company.

Zimmer v McKeithen, 485 F. 2d 1297 (5th Cir. 1973).

Zinn, Howard. 1980. A People's History of the United States. New York: Harper & Row Publishers.

Zukin, Sharon. 1991. Landscapes of Power: From Detroit to Disney World. Berkeley, CA: The University of California Press.

INDEX

Absolutism, 10,22
Abstract, xi,xxvii, 15
Accumulation, xviii,xx,10,14,17-20,22,23, 92
Adam Smith, xiii,9,16 21,23,27,37,43,76,77,92,93
Adjudication, xiv,42
African Americans, xxii,xxx,29,40,45,111, 113,143,144,151,165,169,172,176,180, 184
Alamo Heights Independent School District, 67
Alexander Hamilton, 26,32,34,42,77
Alfred Callaghan, 100
Amorphous, xi
Anarchy, 5,14,15,19,36
Anglos,59,103,135,143,145,146,149,15 3, 157-159,161,170,172,177,189, 184,189
Antonio "Tony" Garza,150
APA, 123
Aperiodic, 84-86,90,97
Articles of Confederation, 32
Attractors, 82,97
Autonomous, 1,5

Bertell Ollman, x
Bexar, 57,58,60,66,127-130,150,158,174,176
Bifurcation point, 79,83,86,95,98,109,117
Boston, 98
Bryan Callaghan, Jr., 99
Bureaucratic, 50,55
Butterfly Effect, 90,91,93

C.B. MacPherson, xiii,13
C.O.P.S., 61
Capitalism, x,xiii,xix,6,8,17,19-22,24,26,28,37,40,43,44,76,81,92,93,18 4,197
Carlos Muñoz, 183

CBD, 102,113,123,132,134
Census Bureau, 29
Chaos theory, 77-82,85-86,88,89,97,107
Charles Beard, xix,26,27
Charles Ornelas, 183
Charles Pinckney, 31,32,34,36,
Chicanos,xxviii,50,52,55,58,59,65,67, 69,74,78,113,117,119,120,122,125,135, 137,183-185
Citizens Organized for Public Service, 61
City council, xxiii,xxv,56,61,62,85,92-94, 100,101,103,104,109-111,113-115, 117,117,118,121,122,125,144,147, 148,152,157,158,165,167,168,170,171, 174,178,179,193-195
City government, xii,xxviii,60,61,72,85,94, 99,101,103,106,111,114,133,174,196
City Public Service Board, 61,127
Civil rights, 35,40,95,151,181
Clarence Thomas, 40
Claus Offe, xxix,48,188
Clinton Rossiter, 29
Colin Powell, 40
Command-type, xxvii
Commission Ring, 100,112
Communist-type, xxvii
Complex,xi,xiv,xvi,xix,xxii,xxvi,40,44, 45,49,55,69,79,87,89,93,177,180,185, 186,193
Complexity, 45,79,83,84,186
Concrete, xi,xii,xiii,xxvii,xxviii
Consolidation,xxxii,116,149,150,152, 171,174-177
Constitution, xix,xxviii,12,26,40-42,68,71, 73
Constitution of the United States, 6,26,27
Constitutional Convention of 1787, xxix
Construct, xii,3,15,16,75,75,77,86,103, 178,179,193
Continental Congress, xix,32
Cornel West, xxii

Novi homini, xiv

Oliver Cromwell, 4
Oscillations, 83
OSHA, 186

Phyllis Schafley, 40
Pluralism, 45,46,102,181
Political incorporation, xxiv,143,191
Political participation,
ix,xxiv,xxxii,24,68,
69,72,154,159,178
Political processes, 28,41,51,98,126,154
Politics,
viii,xxv,2,28,54,60,61,63,68,69,85,
87,98,99,102-108,110,117,149,153,174,
177,177,179,180,185,191
Postmodern, 81
Private, xiv,xxvii,xxix-
xxxi,9,13,18,23,44-
47,49-53,55,56,59,64,65,67,72,76-78,
85,98,102,104-108,112,115,117,119,
123,126,133,138,146,178,178,186-188,
190,192,196,197
Private property, xiv,9,13,18,51,67,197
Public, viii,xiii,xiv,xxii,xxvii,xxix-xxxi,
8,11,14,18,19,22,26,33,34,37-39,41,43,
45-50,53-55,63-65,67,70-72,77,78,89,
90,93,94,96,97,101,104-106,110-112,
116,118,119,123,133,138,146,166,174,
176,179,178,181,182,186,188,189,191,
192,194-196
Public Person, 12

Racial minority,
xx,28,58,121,172,180,182
193
Racially polarized,
xxiii,xxv,xxxii,59,145-
148,150-153,162,164,166,171,194
Racism, xxi,49,59,105,183,191
Ralph Bender, 125
Ralph Miliband, x,89
Raza Unida Party, 102,111
Recharge, 124,193
Reform City, 109
Reform Era, 101,126
Reform Movement, 99
Regimes, 96,117

Representation,
30,31,36,92,152,171,176,
177,194,195
Rivercenter, 132
Robert Blauner, 183
Roger Sherman, 36
Rolling Oaks Mall, 132
Roman Catholic Church, 2

San Antonio, vii,ix,xxi,xxiii-xxv,xxi,
xxxii,53-56,58-64,66,70,72,90,92-95,
97-99,101-113,115-118,119-123, 125
128,130-137,138,143-147,149,151-153,
155,156,158-160,162,164-167,170-178,
180,185,188-194,196-199
Saul Alinsky, 61
Segregation, 53,92,126,180,188,190
Selection, 50,52,53,65,74
Senate, 34,38,150
Service workers, xx
Shavano Park, 132
Sheldon Wolin , 20
Sierra Club, 124
Slaves, 29,30
Social contract, 4,5,9,12
Social psychology, xiv
Social stability, 2,4,5,9,19,24,26
Socialization,
viii,xiii,41,42,49,52,68,69,71,
76,87,153,178,179,185,187
Society,
viii,xii,xiii,xv,xvii,xviii,xxi,xxii,
xxvi,xxviii,xxx,2,4,6,8,9-15,17-22,24,
25,27,28,37,38,40,42,43,44-47,49-53,
66,69-71,73-78,79,81,90,95,97,104,106,
116,120,138,154,180,177,180,181,183-
185,187-189,196-198
Sony Corporation, 106
Sovereign, 4,5,8,9,12,14,15,25,36,85
Spillover Effect
State, viii,ix-xxii,xxiii,xxiv,xxvi,xxviii-
xxxii,1-20,22-25,28,29,31-33,35-39,41-
43,44-48,53,55,56,59,65-67,69,71,75-
79,77-79,81-83,85-90,93,105-107,110,
117,118,119-121,133,140,143,150,152,
155,174,177,179,177,179,180,182,185-
188,190,191,195-199
Static, xii,15,77,86,178,179
Structural arrangements, x,xii,xviii
Structure, viii,x,xv,svii,xix,xxvii,xxxi,

206

STUDIES IN POLITICAL SCIENCE